Towards a Theory of Life-Writing

Towards a Theory of Life-Writing: Genre Blending provides a look into the rules of life-writing genre blending proposing a theory to explain and illustrate the main regulations governing such genre play. It centers on fact and fiction duality in the formation of auto/biofictional genres. This book investigates the existing developments in this field and explores major criticism and lines of inquiry in order to arrive at the theory of life-writing genre play textuality. The specific interplay of the different generic characteristics develops a specific textuality at the heart of it. This is termed biofictional preservation (biopreservation) to explain the textual transformation and the shaping of the auto/biofictional genres. Written for undergraduate and graduate students, but also for the general readers, the book further exemplifies the theory in the analyses of different biofictions about the American authors F. Scott Fitzgerald and Ernest Hemingway featuring overlapping and juxtaposed material. This volume aims to provide a theory of this specific textuality in order to better understand and approach the process in question as well as to open up new horizons for further study and exploration.

Marija Krsteva holds a PhD degree in American literature from the Sofia University "St. Kliment Ohridski" in Bulgaria. Her area of interest involves American studies, history, culture and literature, mainly contemporary literature, life-writing and genre blending. She has worked at the University "Goce Delcev" in Stip, Faculty of Philology since 2012 where she teaches American studies. Marija Krsteva is a Hemingway Society fellow for 2017.

Routledge Auto/Biography Studies
Series Editor: Ricia A. Chansky

Trans Narratives
Trans, Transmedia, Transnational
Edited by Ana Horvat, Orly Lael Netzer, Sarah McRae and Julie Rak

Speculative Biography
Experiments, Opportunities and Provocations
Edited by Donna Lee Brien and Kiera Lindsey

Memoirs of Race, Color, and Belonging
Nicole Stamant

Engaging Donna Haraway
Lives in the Natureculture Web
Edited by Cynthia Huff and Margaretta Jolly

Afropean Female Selves
Migration and Language in the Life Writing of Fatou Diome and Igiaba Scego
Christopher Hogarth

Artists and Their Autobiographies from Today to the Renaissance and Back
Symptoms of Sincerity
Charles Reeve

Towards a Theory of Life-Writing
Genre Blending
Marija Krsteva

For more information about this series, please visit: www.routledge.com/Routledge-Auto-Biography-Studies/book-series/AUTO

Towards a Theory of Life-Writing
Genre Blending

Marija Krsteva

NEW YORK AND LONDON

First published 2023
by Routledge
605 Third Avenue, New York, NY 10158

and by Routledge
4 Park Square, Milton Park, Abingdon, Oxon, OX14 4RN

Routledge is an imprint of the Taylor & Francis Group, an informa business

© 2023 Marija Krsteva

The right of Marija Krsteva to be identified as author of this work has been asserted in accordance with sections 77 and 78 of the Copyright, Designs and Patents Act 1988.

All rights reserved. No part of this book may be reprinted or reproduced or utilised in any form or by any electronic, mechanical, or other means, now known or hereafter invented, including photocopying and recording, or in any information storage or retrieval system, without permission in writing from the publishers.

Trademark notice: Product or corporate names may be trademarks or registered trademarks, and are used only for identification and explanation without intent to infringe.

ISBN: 978-1-032-35642-6 (hbk)
ISBN: 978-1-032-35644-0 (pbk)
ISBN: 978-1-003-32779-0 (ebk)

DOI: 10.4324/9781003327790

Typeset in Times New Roman
by codeMantra

Contents

	Introduction	1
1	**Postmodern genre play**	14
	1.1 Genre in literature 14	
	1.2 Genre play in postmodern writing 18	
2	**Auto/biography and literature**	26
	2.1 Literary biography 26	
	2.2 Biopreservation: the building block of postmodern literary biography 36	
3	**F. Scott Fitzgerald and Ernest Hemingway as fictional characters**	42
	3.1 Fictionalizing Hemingway 42	
	3.2 Fictionalizing Fitzgerald 46	
4	**Narrative identity and image building in *Z: A Novel of Zelda Fitzgerald***	50
5	**Narrative identity and image building in *The Paris Wife***	70
	Conclusion	97
	Bibliography	101
	Index	113

Introduction

> All biographies, like all autobiographies, like all narratives tell one story in place of another.
> – Helene Cixous

The field of life-writing genre play has been exponentially developing during the twentieth century, reaching the forefront of the main literary tendencies in the twenty-first century. As such, it has proven to be quite complex and in need of a bigger academic attention. The present book aims to respond to the major challenges in the field and propose a viable literary theory that would explain and establish the position of the genre of biofiction in contemporary literature. To that end, this book studies the most prominent debates in all the literary forms resulting from the life-writing genre play such as biographical fictions, autobiographical fictions and literary biographies. Following a close examination of the narrative sequences in the novelistic rewritings of the lives of two of America's most notable authors, Ernest Hemingway and F. Scott Fitzgerald, the book provides a theory on the life-writing genre play textuality. It reveals the specific textual and narrative transformation resulting from the fact and fiction duality pertinent to biographical fictions. The book gives sufficient examples of life stories that have been repeatedly used as plot lines in postmodern biofictions, which, it should be noted, underline the connection between fiction, biography and autobiography by developing texts that are "both self-reflexive and yet paradoxically also lay claim to historical events and personages" (Hutcheon 2003:5). The process of creating such texts involves different appropriations of facts, fictional characters, literary works and practices, themes and subjects, which are re-ordered in a constantly changing world of doubling, mirror reflections and fluctuations constructing in this way narrative identities that subvert the popularly accepted images of public figures.

This creative process, known as life-writing genre play is a never-ending intriguing constructive dialogue between fact and fiction. As a result, new terms and varieties of genres keep on emerging such as: autofiction (a term Serge Dubrowski coined in 1977; Philipe Villain distinguishes it from autobiographical novel in that it requires the first-person narrator who is also a protagonist to be the same as the author) autobiografiction (a concept first coined by Stephen Reynolds in 1906, further researched and developed by Max Saunders as combining and blurring of all different life-writing forms, of fiction in autobiography and autobiography in fiction), factual metaautobiogrpahy (according to Christina Struth the term designates a relatively new development within autobiographical writing that reflects on its own conditions and conventions, the history of autobiography and contemporary autobiographical practices), metabiography (a term used to denote the relation between the biographee and the social, historical, temporal cultural and economic circumstances of the biographer), autotopography (critic Jennifer Gonzalez sees autotopography as a way to study how a person's integral objects become, overtime, so intrinsic to telling one's story), autre-biography (defined as a metafictional autobiography, which emphasizes the themes of subject, identity and power, as well as historiographic metafiction), heterobiography (defined by Boldrini as fictional autobiographies of historical individuals), biofiction (literature with a protagonist named after a real-life person, and the author fictionalizes that historical figure in order to show a common theme between otherwise unlike things or to convey a larger meaning, such as for social commentary), fictional biography (a genre wherein an author writes an account of a person's life where that person is actually a fictional character), literary biography (the biographical exploration of the lives of writers and artists) and the list could go on. This proliferation, while enriching, seems to pose considerable issues on all levels of literary, cultural and philosophical criticism. In the analytical part, we can see the interplay of different elements forming all the above generic varieties.

To begin with, one of the best examples of this "mixing of genres" comes from the field of literary biography. As Michael Benton (2009) points out, it is important to always keep in mind the documentary aspect of writing about somebody's life, but since the meaning assigned to the study of facts becomes mixed with fiction, the genre falls into the postmodern category of historiographic metafiction. Thus, such a study establishes the relation as one of a reading that is not just a collection of information about someone's life but a complex combination of factual and fictional elements. It further explores the convincing aspect of this final product, how much it adheres to the theoretical postulates about life-writing and how much it can be located in a particular theoretical frame. The juxtaposition of the main elements of the different types of the writing explains the nature of making a metafictional modification, a historiographical-metafictional modification in the development of literary biography. The subgenre's internal representational devices then become subject to exploration of historiographic metafictional elements (Benton 2009:38).

In particular, historiographic metafiction unveils the theme of life-writing acknowledging the postmodern worldview as the convention of the period. As Benton suggests, it is exactly this feature of historiographic metafiction, the concentration on intertextual and parodical building of scenes and stories that becomes one of the fundamental concerns in defining the genre of literary biography. That is why he focuses on the representation of the duality of history and fiction, craft and art, the life and the works, and on the resulting hybridity of literary biography. He believes that it is the postmodern aesthetic that "establishes significant facts" and at the same time reveals "stories", while the success of the author of a literary biography lies in their ability to select and re-arrange the material designing the life stories of their characters thus creating "biomythographies" (Benton 2009:53). This claim is in line with Cohn's urge to draw a line on what is fictional and what is factual, or to define the "signposts of fictionality" (Cohn 1990).

It is in this sense that this book analyzes the narrative techniques used by the different postmodern writers to create new genre forms in life-writing. These forms are usually closely connected to the processes of hybridization, bending of boundaries and blending of characteristics. In other words, what this book intends to reveal is how the genre play has become an inherent feature of postmodern writing, often associated with specific forms of textuality. Moreover, this textuality emerges as the theoretical foundation for study and analysis of biofictions, thus filling the existing gap of specific theory on life-writing genre play.

It should be noted that biofictions and genre play have had their variations in literature throughout the centuries. The most recent trends in biofictional writing reflect the global changes of the twentieth and twenty-first centuries and therefore they are most conveniently situated in the postmodern paradigm. It is worth considering that in line with such global changes come the reactions to postmodernism in the form of post-postmodern trends or metamodernism. According to Timotheus Vermeulen and Robin van den Akker (2010), the new postmodern sensibility oscillates between and beyond modern positions and postmodern strategies. The term *meta* here refers to Plato's *metaxy* to denote a movement between opposite poles as well as beyond and not to reflective stance or repetition. It is possible that the biofictional trend might be situated within such trends as a reply to different developments such as climate change, the financial crisis and (geo)political instability but also digital trends and technological advancements. Still, the core strategies could be recognized as postmodern or postmodern variations.

In order to arrive at the proposed theoretical framework within which all these different forms of textuality in the field of literary biography can be critically interpreted, the book analyzes in detail two of the postmodern biofictions about F. Scott Fitzgerald's and Ernest Hemingway's lives rather curiously concentrating not on the two male writers but on the women in their lives: *Z: A Novel of Zelda Fitzgerald* (2013) by Therese Ann Fowler and *The Paris Wife* (2011) by Paula McLain. As an additional source of interpretation, another biofiction, *Hemingway's Girl* (2012) by Erika Robuck is used, as a way of strengthening the argument. The study compares and contrasts these works with Zelda Fitzgerald's own semi-autobiographical novel *Save Me the Waltz* (1932) and Marta Gellhorn's autobiographical travelogue, *Travels with Myself and Another* (1978). The comparison serves the purpose of illustrating the specific image-making that takes place in the biofictions as a result of the unique narrative identities developed in the texts. Thus, it also aims to prove that postmodern fiction of the early twenty-first century allows the multi-genre play to undermine the established hierarchies and patterns of behavior, especially those of a male-dominated world.

The three biofictions, analyzed in light of genre blending, or what may also be called "genre play", hybridization (Hutcheon 2003), "creolization" (Anderson 1991) and blending (Benton 2009), provide the basis of formulating a new perspective through which postmodern life-writing can be understood. I call this a process of biofictional preservation, or "biopreservation". I use the term "biopreservation" to refer to the "literary" preservation of one's life, and "bio" to refer to the facts of one's life. Biopreservation can be viewed as an experiment with different postmodern modes and techniques of writing, as a play with generic characteristics. Similar to the process of biopreservation in biochemical laboratories, in the process of literary creation, the authors decide which facts from the biography of their subjects and which traits of their characters they want to preserve and then choose what "literary" "preservatives" to use to create the fictional stories. The end product is a biofiction that illustrates a new vision of the past times. Thus, the term metaphorically refers to the scientific process of biopreservation denoting the unique genre play in postmodern rewriting of the lives of historical figures. I see the work of this process in the dynamics of the text and by finding, describing and explaining the main elements of biopreservation, I try to establish a theoretical foundation for explaining the genre play in biofictions. Interestingly, the terms "genre" and "hybridization" also take root in natural sciences and find their way in humanities.

The need for such a study has arisen from the lack of a specific theory dealing with the formation and implications of this new genre in terms of its specific characteristics and textuality. The biggest online network of books and readers, Goodreads harbors numerous works of blended life-writing genres, however, most of these works are either wrongly labeled or little investigated which might obstruct the attempt to review or understand the work in the best possible light. The situation is not less complicated in academic research and study. While many excellent attempts to uncover the main characteristics of the genre have been made in this field, no specific theory has been proposed that would reveal the governing structures of the life-writing genre play on a textual level. Therefore, this particular textuality could be considered an initial point in all further studies and analyses of a work of biofiction.

Adding to the need to critically address such genre blending is Gérard Genette's exploration of the factual and fictional in his essay "Fictional Narrative, Factual Narrative" from Fiction&Diction where he examines the notions of order, pace, frequency, mood and voice in light of factual and fictional narratives. He concludes that "if we consider actual practices, we have to admit that there is no such thing as pure fiction and no such thing as history so rigorous that it abjures any 'emplotting' and any use of novelistic techniques" (Genette 1993:82). He further urges the need to explore the rules behind this mixture saying

6 Introduction

> Indeed, the question ought to be all the less discouraging to empirical inquiry, for even -or especially- if narrative forms readily cross the borderline between fiction and non-fiction, it is no less urgent, or rather it is all the more urgent, for narratology to follow this example.
>
> (Genette 1993:84)

Therefore, the aim of this book is to determine the specific type of textuality as a key aspect and a starting point in the analysis of such narratives since the generic interconnectedness and the inevitable contact between the factual and the fictional calls for such an approach.

In this respect, I isolate and describe the main characteristics of the biopreservation process in the above biofictions. The analytical approach establishes the theory and draws general conclusions about the role of biopreservation in genre blending. Furthermore, I use biopreservation to show how the (auto)biofictional narrative identities of the women around the two modernist writers are constructed and how that shapes the images of F. Scott Fitzgerald and Ernest Hemingway. Similarly, other analyses could be made to other biofictions, inspired from different socio-cultural and historical aspects they want to convey.

I first discuss the blending of the traditional critical theory and creative practices and outline new insights into the theory and the craft of contemporary postmodern fiction. This stages a practical and theoretical inquiry into the double, hybrid functions of the texts as historical and literary. In this respect, the study offers a novel interpretation of how life-writing influences the genre conventions of fiction, biography and autobiography, the creative process and the negotiating of the self and the relation between the reader and the author in a wider social and historical context. These works of fiction exhibit the capacity of the postmodern novel to project the characteristics of historiographic metafiction. They are composite texts that dramatize key events in the apparently disparate lives of the writers turned subjects. The accent here is on the process of how different themes surrounding the writers' lives are reworked in the fictional space.

One of the specific traits of this study that serves the theory of biopreservation, derives from the formation of Zelda and Hadley's fictional narrative identities, as well as from the depiction of Fitzgerald and Hemingway as characters in postmodern fiction seen as the result of genre transgression and the use of postmodern techniques of writing. I specifically look into the process of subverting and debunking the mythical figures of the writers and into the possibility of an assertion of new portraits of the writers' lives. For the first time in novelistic writing, the figures of Fitzgerald and Hemingway do not take central part. Instead, it is their wives that get the central place in these life stories, and it is through their voices that these stories are heard. Thus, the characters of the two authors are presented from their wives' perspectives. This study shows how the postmodern genre play dismisses a singular dominating perspective and introduces a new, female one, which becomes as important as the conventional, male perspective as it is presented in the volume of critical studies and biographies of the two modernist writers.

The paradigm, therefore, consists of a combination of the postmodern theories of narrative, literary biography and narrative identity. The organizational structure includes the historical period and the aesthetic movement as well as the strategies of writing and the theoretical assumptions which allows me to handle and interpret the texts in a comparative analysis. For this purpose, a various and diverse toolbox is organized around an enduring critical discussion of the relation between a literary text and the theories relevant to its composition. The close reading of the books looks into the language, structure and form unifying and dis-unifying the repositories of meanings rendered by the texts. Centered on the textual formation, this study reveals a new correspondence between different fictional and non-fictional genres. Investigating the goals and tools of auto/biographical and postmodern writing, the analytical account unravels the genre play at the center of these texts and demonstrates their construction and the new realities they create.

I begin with an outline of the concept of genre in terms of a way of understanding, structuring and ordering of human experience and the understanding of the world in general. The theoretical account involves a critical analysis of the views of theoreticians such as Mikhail Bakhtin (1981), Northrop Frye (1957) and Gerrard Genette (1992) as well as John Swales (1990) and Daniel Chandler (1997). The theoretical review is presented in light of genre's predisposition to modification and genre play and not so much in an attempt to exhaust all the existing scholarship on literary genres. In addition to that, I also look closely at the views on the genre of life-writing of theoreticians such as Saunders (2010), Schwalm (2014), Eakin (1985) and Nünning (2005).

Furthermore, the analysis draws on Linda Hutcheon's theoretical concepts presented in *A Poetics of Postmodernism: History,*

Theory, Fiction (2003). The study of the three novels offers insights into the framework of the postmodernist creative process in which as Hutcheon (2003) claims metafiction is usually equated with the postmodern practice of creating a text showing its own structure, talking about itself and demonstrating itself as a fiction. This is a process in which postmodern authors ask readers for their active participation. The willing suspension of disbelief is no longer required as they do not have to be passively involved in the fictitious world of the postmodern, which does not necessarily resemble the real world. These novelists explore a contingent reality and not a structured one. This can be ascribed to the critical interest in history and the rewriting of history in postmodern literary practice through the combination of historiography and metafiction in "historiographic metafiction".

According to Hutcheon (2003), historiographic metafiction uses metafiction to accentuate the construction of history, producing a literary artifact. Metafiction draws attention to the fact that the past is understood by texts which are always intertextual. At the same time, the world and reality are perceived as products of culture and their representations in different narratives are what build our knowledge of the world. Therefore, postmodernism turns to one of the fundamental techniques of knowing the world, intertextuality. What is more, it is through intertextual parody that the world and its past are presented in these postmodern texts, i.e. the past is still incorporated in the present but questioned in parody. In Hutcheon's view, parody is the very essence of postmodernism: "Parody—often called ironic quotation, pastiche, appropriation, or intertextuality—is usually considered central to postmodernism, both by its detractors and its defenders" (1989:93). In her understanding, it is a way of both legitimizing and subverting what it parodies, forming the connection between past and present events.

In this sense, according to Hutcheon (1985), if parody is a postmodern technique that aims to give ironic representation of genre and ideology by questioning and unsettling the established beliefs and world views, then by means of intertextual parody postmodern texts take the form of self-conscious, self-reflexive historiographic metafiction. As an example of that, we can see the biofictions about F. Scott Fitzgerald and Ernest Hemingway and the women around them that are in the focus of my study. However, in postmodern life-writing due to the genre play, parody and intertextuality assume different attributes as my own theoretical proposition shows.

Generally speaking, contemporary self-reflexive historiographic metafiction subverts the view of history as a coherent inscription of unified subjectivity. The questions of how the issues of narrative representation, textuality, subjectivity and ideology are dealt with in the postmodern combinations of fiction, non-fiction and history are the centers of this investigation. To reach an answer, I rely not only on Hutcheon's ideas but also on Jaroslav Kušnír's interpretation of postmodern writings as developed in his study *Postmodernism in American and Australian Fiction* (2011) as well as on the classification of the narrative elements provided by David Herman in his book *Basic Elements of the Narrative* (2009), on Dan P. McAdams's and Kate C. McLean's view of how the narrative identity is constructed (2013 and 2008) and on the ideas of McAdams, Josselson and Lieblich concerning the creation of narrative selves in their *Identity and Story: Creating Self in Narrative* (2008), and finally on the two book-length studies of the genre of the literary biography Michael Benton, *Literary Biography, An Introduction* (2009) and *Towards a Poetics of Literary Biography* (2015). All these studies examine the authors' use of the conventions of the narrative and genre and their subversion in postmodern writings in view of historical reference, subjectivity and ideology in the textual and cultural contexts.

It is in this sense that postmodern challenges to historicity and historiographic metafiction most clearly overlap with the postmodern concerns of narratology as developed by Tzvetan Todorov, Roland Barthes, A.-J. Greimas, Paul Ricouer and Hayden White (Onega et al. 2014). For the purposes of this study, however, I use primarily Gérard Genette's theory of intertextuality as part of his poetics of narratology, McAdams's elements of narrative identity as well as David Herman's narrative elements. According to Herman, a narrative can be seen as a cognitive structure or a way of making sense of experience, a type of text and as a resource for communicative interaction. The working definition of a narrative, he suggests, is "rather than focusing on general abstract situations and trends, stories are an account of what happened to particular people – and what it was like to for them to experience what happened – in particular circumstances and with specific consequences" (Herman 2009:2).

The biofictions of F. Scott Fitzgerald and Ernest Hemingway offer a broad playing field for exploring these processes in view of their constitutive elements. They also cause a specific cultural effect of wanting to read and write a biofiction that presents a novel narrative form which is spiced up with the introduction of little-known facts about the public figures and their literary characters. Biofictions also show how the apparent limitations of writing about a person's life inevitably lay claim to the choices individuals make and how the new genre is born as a consequence of the desire to interpret and reflect on these choices from the point of view of the novelist. This study reveals how this goal is achieved by the specific genre play in the text.

All this adds to another important aspect of biofictional writing, the establishment of a specific relationship between the author, the subject and culture. What happens is that the writer presents the relationship to the reader in various degrees of transparency, since the subject, as part of both factual and fictional narratives, is inevitably influenced by what the reader knows about them. Herman's narrative theory and the analysis of the way in which the biofiction authors use postmodern literary modes and techniques help to detect the emphatic points in the meaning-making where fact and fiction come into contact. Sometimes these points signal the existence of "hidden subjects" in biofictional works which ask the question of what is omitted in one story and what is emphasized in another. That is how F. Scott Fitzgerald and Ernest Hemingway can be cast into the roles of fictional characters whose function is to make readers figure out their wives' narrative identities.

The paradigm of the study comprises all of the above theoretical concepts and allows me to analyze and explain my findings. The unit of the analysis has been defined as a textual unit called a "biopreservation sequence". This can be seen as the smallest unit of the genre play. The biopreservation sequence is a textual element that forms part of a narrative element and consists of both factual (archived) and fictional parts. It is transformative and revolutionary, constructing, revising and appropriating different meanings and image presentations. Typically, the biopreservation sequence shapes the narrative presentations of the self, as well as the plot structure out of the predictable situations, episodes, obstacles, conflicts, resolutions, stereotypes, roles, personal qualities, motivations, goals, behavior, themes, topics, subject matter, social, cultural, psychological, professional, political, sexual and moral values, geographical and historical setting and tone available to the author and thus builds up an element of the narrator's identity. As a result, biofictions contain numerous biopreservation sequences forming a constellation of meanings all participating actively in the shaping of the image of the biographee. Finally, they define afresh what has already been established in past narratives.

In its nature, biopreservation can also be seen as an intertextual subtype specific to the creation of hybrid genres, combining biography and fiction. As such, biopreservation metafictionally constructs and inscribes the self, the truth and reality. It does so by invention. Biopreservation completes what seems incomplete and genre transformation would be impossible without it. It is in this sense that texts are created by means of intertextuality which, as a consequence, creates the whole context.

The biopreservation sequence as the generator of the genre play is what makes the text interactive. Genres become adaptive to different goals and perspectives in revisiting and restating the life stories being told. We explore the biopreservation sequences arising from the fact and fiction duality in the biofictions about F. Scott Fitzgerald and Ernest Hemingway. Most notably, these sequences establish the reflecting and refracting images of the biographees. By comparing the images and the narrative identities in the biofictions with those in the books of the biographees' wives, I investigate how much of the incurred meaning is a product of subjectivity, popular culture or creativity. The study discusses any possible constraints or declinations in the narrative of the self and what the role of biopreservation in this respect entails. It shows how the biopreservation sequences have the potential to establish "famous authors' schemata", or image-making and thus point to the possibility of establishing similar conventions in the three biofictions discussed here.

Furthermore, since biopreservation sequences can show how any event or a piece of information is connected with the emerging narratives of the self, the analysis looks into the most widely known and the least-known narratives associated with the lives of the two iconic literary figures noting the difference. It illustrates how the biopreservation sequences influence the whole narrative in the respective biofictions. Finally, this confirms my claim that biopreservation can serve as a solution to the contextual and creative challenges in postmodern life-writing.

The structure of the work is divided into a theoretical part and an ensuing analytical one. Chapter 1 looks into the concept of genre and genre theories. The concept of genre is examined in light of its potential to offer different interpretations and its open nature for variations. This part establishes the grounds of my theoretical framework and its subsequent use in the analysis of the literary works by outlining the potential of genres to blend and create new meanings. Therefore, the stress of the second part of this chapter falls on the postmodern traits reflected in contemporary genre blending. This approach inevitably leads to postmodernist investigation, i.e. of testing the genre's activities in postmodernist conditions. It proves necessary to present the postmodernist concepts crucial to genre blending or at least to genre changes. This discussion unravels a more detailed theoretical review that draws on the connection between genre blending and the postmodernist problematics of fact and fiction duality.

Chapter 2 investigates one such instance of genre blending, i.e. the literary biography. The chapter explores the existing scholarship on literary biography, the main conclusions and areas of investigation. It further gives a critical review on all existing scholarship on life-writing genre blending, in particular, on the newly formed genre of biofiction. This paves the way to deriving the theory of biopreservation and the analytical account of the biofictions subject to my study. It leads to the next part of this chapter aimed to present the concept of biopreservation as integral to the process of genre hybridization and the formation of the new genre of biofiction. The study argues that biopreservation is an essential aspect of the biofictions' textuality. Furthermore, it shows how the genre play establishes the fictional narratives of famous persons in history. Accordingly, this chapter concludes a broad eclectic field that is both taking a momentum and is dynamic, thus sparking a ceaseless interest in its inherent rules and regulations.

Chapter 3 is entirely devoted to the critical review of the existing biographies, strictly factual and more fictional, published about F. Scott Fitzgerald and Ernest Hemingway. The chapter further underlines the necessity for establishing a viable theory on this increasingly popular literary genre. Both the public and the academia are caught in the midst of the creative process, the cultural and literary developments of the time and the unprecedented availability of information and global communication. While this fosters understanding, it can also lead to possible misunderstandings or confusions on how to categorize similar narratives. When looked closer, the life-writing narratives seem to rise a never-ending inquiry as to how and what they portray.

Chapter 4 shows how the biopreservation process works in practice, in constructing the image of F. Scott Fitzgerald in the biofictional narrative presented in the form of a fictional autobiographical account of his wife *Zelda in Z: A Novel of Zelda Fitzgerald* contrasted with real Zelda's own semi-autobiography, *Save Me the Waltz*. This particular contrasting of the two narratives aims to get hold of the internal textual changes and transformations before the final product is reached. By means of dissecting the biopreservational sequences, the chapter details the narrative elements that form and shape an equally unique life-writing genre, equally valuable and intriguing as the next one. The comparison, however, enables numerous conclusions on the meaning the narrative aims to convey, such as the building of the fictional narrative self of the real-life wife of F. Scott Fitzgerald, Zelda Fitzgerald.

Similarly, Chapter 5, critically analyzes the biopreservation process taking place in the narratives about Ernest Hemingway, *The Paris Wife*, *Travels with Myself and Another* and *Hemingway's Girl*. This analysis unravels Hadley's narrative identity and the creation of Hemingway's biofictional image. This, in turn, is compared with the biofictions about Fitzgerald from the previous chapter. Again, the concept of biopreservation is used to examine the life-writing textuality resulting from the mixture of the genre.

In the conclusion, the study outlines the major theoretical concepts arising from the analysis and confirms the necessity for the concept of biopreservation in understanding contemporary biofictional narratives. The separate chapters provide separate aspects of the complex field of life-writing genre play. They gradually lead to the core thesis, and that is the necessity for a literary theory of life-writing genre play, namely, on the genre of biofiction. The theoretical part and the subsequent analysis prove that only by investigating on the inside one can understand what is on the outside.

1 Postmodern genre play

1.1 Genre in literature

As one of the most innate human characteristics, creativity is also an all-encompassing recourse when it comes to human development in general. In its essence, creativity is also an experiment naturally belonging to genre play. Biofiction authors are no exempt from this. Their inherent deftness places them in-between genre rules and conventions and creative spurts trying to make the "best of both", and it is in the genre play that they exert their power and creative potential.

Genres exist in all spheres of life. They represent a way of conceptualizing the world, establishing order and providing understanding. Accordingly, in the world of postmodernism too, genres take their rightful place as shaping elements of human experience. Since the world is constantly changing, genres are also changing in response. Despite having recognizable structural and organizational patterns, genres and their composition become affected by current movements. Therefore, genre theories are also trying to respond to the challenging flexibility of genres. In doing so, they all show different perspectives in categorizing genres according to their different goals. Broadly speaking, genre theories and genre studies encompass the fields of linguistics, rhetorics, art and literature and they all try to grasp the essence of genre as a category. Together with film and cultural criticism, literary theory in general takes on the structuralist approach to understanding genre, in finding patterns in different works of art. When a set of recognizable patterns recur and become prevalent in a piece of art, that piece assumes the status of a certain genre.

The underlying assumption is that genres exist only with human beings as social beings and therefore cannot be separated from a social action. The term genre (in French *genre* meaning "kind", "type" or "class", Latin *genus*) involves a certain degree of classification, typification and taxonomy. There are various distinguishing criteria in the formation of genre classification. Usually, a literary genre is classified into a certain group according to its structure, form, tone, organization, literary technique, style and content. According to this, various synchronic and diachronic classification systems have been developed. However, the greater the number of criteria, the less absolute the system is. A literary work is imbued with semiotic codes that are transcoded by means of all of these criteria. As a result, the new genre piece is never absolutely fixed to one group due to the variability of the semiotic codes across the criteria. One piece can belong to one genre according to a literary technique and to another one according to organization and content. This is where both the rich creative potential of genre and its elusiveness lie.

For the purposes of my own study, I look into some of the prevailing definitions of the genre within the literary field. When in 1976 Tsvetan Todorov wrote, "To persist in discussing genres today might seem like an idle if not obviously anachronistic pastime" (1976:159), he seemed to have captured the spirit of the oncoming postmodern age. But still, even today, the debate about the true nature of the genre has not ceased. Basing his argument on the re-reading of Blanchot's *Le livre à venir* (1959), Todorov claims that "the fact that a work 'disobeys' its genre does not make the latter nonexistent" (1976:160). "Therefore, it is not 'genres' that have disappeared, but the genres of the past, and they have been replaced by others", he concludes (1976:169). Thus, for the present study, he reaches an important conclusion that "a new genre is always the transformation of one of several old genres: by inversion, by displacement, by combination" (1976:161). It is exactly this process that I try to follow in the books I discuss and see what has made possible the birth of the new genre of biofiction and how we can define it.

Of course, in order to proceed with that line of investigation, an answer to the question "What is a genre?" seems due. Such scholars as the American literary critic Wayne C. Booth in his *The Rhetoric of Fiction* (1961) and the Canadian literary theoretician Northrop Frye position genre in a system of categories and connect it closely with rhetoric. In his fourth essay, "Rhetorical Criticism: Theory of Genre", Frye discusses genre within the intersection of three main areas: one involving art, beauty, feeling and taste, the second one of social actions and events, and the third one of individual thought (Frye 1957:243–245). He merges this study with rhetoric (as ornamental persuasive speech), which he considers integral to the analysis. When it comes to genre and tropes, Frye considers the relations between tropes and genres necessary in the genre study.

> The dynamic behind the generic modeling of discourse derives from tropes, conceived not or not simply as a system of classification, a rule of ornament or a recipe for persuasion but as constituting a fundamental cognitive faculty of the mind.
>
> (Frye, 1992:5)

Todorov, however, provides an answer that is very much informed by his re-readings not only of Blanchot but of the semiotician Charles Morris and finally of Mikhail Bakhtin. Bakhtin's genre theory rotates around the idea of genre's creative potential. According to him, the creation of a new text, or a new genre for that matter, is a new situation, a new event (Bakhtin 1981:171–324). Bakhtin maintains that a dialogic work of literature is in contrast with a monologic one. The dialogic work constantly resurges in and out of other texts, works of literature and authors. It does not simply involve modifications such as correction, extension or silencing of another work, but constantly informs and is informed by other texts. These theoretical postulates show the complexity of individual texts as always involving multiple voices and therefore multiple genre echoes in their creation. Ultimately, genre for Bakhtin is a "constitutive factor in the production of textuality" (Bakhtin 1981:280).

Todorov's definition is closely linked to Bakhtin's ideas but concentrates on the different levels of the discourse:

> A genre, literary or otherwise, is nothing but the codification of discursive properties [...] These properties arise either from the semantic aspect of the text, or from its syntactic aspect [...], or from the pragmatic aspect [...], or finally from the verbal aspect.
>
> (Todorov 1976:162–163)

A similar approach to define what the genre is can be found in the work of John Swales. His ideas on genre analysis tackle genre in relation to "discourse community" and "language learning". According to him, genre analysis can be used to understand "the myriad communicative events that occur in the contemporary English-speaking academy" (Swales 1990:1). His approach tries to identify key aspects of language learning by genres as "communicative events", consisting of spoken or written texts or a combination of both within "discourse communities" as "sociorhetorical networks in order to work towards sets of common goals" (Swales 1990:9). He further specifies the existence of specific "content schemata" or knowledge of prior texts and "formal schemata" which learners develop in order to acquire their language skills.

This structuralist view of the genre has been challenged in more recent times by critics who insist on the social action that stands behind each attempt to define a genre. As Robert Hodge and Gunther Kress claim, "genres only exist in so far as a social group declares and enforces the rules that constitute them" (Chandler 1997:7). Thus, for them the genre's form and content are determined by characteristics and repeated social actions fulfilling certain goals. In this respect, genres are the result of social actions that individuals turn into texts. Carolyn Miller argues that "a rhetorically sound definition of genre must be centered not on the substance of form of discourse but on the action it is used to accomplish" (Miller 1984:151). Gunther Kress defines a genre as "a kind of text that derives its form from the structure of a frequently repeated social occasion with its characteristic participants and their purposes" (Kress 1988:183). Each new text has the potential of hybridity, i.e. influencing the changes in the genre and the creation of new genre types. As Jacques Derrida suggests, "there is no genre-less text" (Derrida 1980:65). Furthermore, according to Katie Wales, genre is an intertextual concept (Wales 1989:259). Human experience is shaped in the interaction between different texts, and as Roland Barthes (1975) puts it, it is genre that makes sense of certain events within a text. John Hartley suggests that "we need to understand genre as the property of relations between texts" (O'Sullivan et al. 1994:128).

This attempt to see the genre as closely tied to the interaction between texts and textual practices has been furthered by Gérard Genette who has created a novel structural narratology in an attempt to reflect the new challenges in narratological poetics. He believes that it is necessary to provide new definitions so that they would suit new objects and tendencies.

> From the ancient thought the medieval Renaissance, Enlightenment and Romantic, and on, the modern theories of literary genre, Genette traces the process by which new forms of textuality are regularly justified by being assigned ancient

lineages, the thicket of poetics thus continually made denser and more difficult to penetrate. His project is to prime this thicket and blaze trails through it.

(Genette 1992: viii)

Revising the founding tripartite system of Plato and Aristotle, Genette forms the idea of genres as intersections of certain modes of enunciation (persistent to linguistics) and certain thematic concerns (although also persistent, still greatly influenced by culture and society) (Genette 1992: viii). "Modes and themes, intersecting, jointly include and determine genres" (Genette, 1992:73). In his renewed poetics, Genette is mostly interested in textual transcendence, namely, "everything that brings it into relation (manifest or hidden) with other texts" (Genette 1992:80). He calls that transtextuality. This concept includes intertextuality, according to Kristeva's idea of one text's presence within another. Then there is metatextuality modeling it on language/metalanguage as a transtextual relationship linking text to its comments, something all literary critics have employed (Genette 1992:82). The other two concepts involve paratextuality, as all the accompanying parts of one text (such as additional information, a written foreword, photos, etc.) and architextuality, "that relationship of inclusion that links each text to the various types of discourse it belongs to" (Genette 1992:82).

My own concept of textual transcendence, exemplified by the concept of biopreservation, can be seen as yet another link in the above chain of theories. Biopreservation as a process of textual transformation, however, can be most clearly recognized within the postmodern paradigm, although not exclusively. To see how postmodernism affects such textuality and enables genre play, we need to look into the major traits of postmodernism.

1.2 Genre play in postmodern writing

Investigation into the genre's laws is no less complex than the genre's creative nature itself. This is especially evident in the case of biofiction writers who have to take on a double task of being both a "biographer" and a "fiction writer". That also raises a number of compelling issues when it comes to narration and narrative identity since these writers very consciously embark on the difficult task of balancing between factual and fictional representations of famous public figures. On the surface, these narratives seem to be marked by clear oppositions. On the one hand, there is the pertinent presence of the biography as an established genre, and on the other, there is the inevitable imposition of fiction's creative potential. The biofiction authors avail themselves of these "opposing concepts" and summon into action a unique genre play.

"Play" is the central characteristic of the textual formations and in the use of narrative techniques in postmodern writing in general and biofictions in particular. It should be underlined that the theories about play and games have varied throughout the centuries, but they have all maintained that playing is essential to human experience, especially when it comes to the use of language.

> For some, the play of language is Plato's 'mere play', a fooling with language and other cultural activities without particular rules, structures and goals. For others, the unclosed and unstructured play of language and texts leads to new structures and goals; in brief to games instead of play. For still others, the play is not 'mere' play at all, but neither is it game.
> (Slethaug 1993:30)

In addition, another term, world-play, sees all human activity as part of a play.

> The world-play at its decentering is drawn from theories of play by Friedrich Nietzsche and Martin Heidegger who conclude that each of us is responsible not only for transgressing and disrupting current cultural attitudes, beliefs and codes, but also for taking the responsibility of setting our own goals and drawing up our individual rules of belief and conduct.
> (Slethaug 1993:30)

Playfulness has become an omnipresent aspect in human's existence, but I am particularly interested in how language discloses playfulness in postmodern fiction. My specific interest is to examine the postmodern genre play crucial to the rewriting of the lives of historical figures. For this purpose, I look into the ways genres interact, the liminality of the biofictional form, and the tools and techniques used in the process of that interaction.

The work of the biofiction author is that of a creative scientist performing a literary experiment. The author follows the obvious principles of organization of the narrative genres in use, but the way the narrative starts to interact with these principles, changes and transforms them, results in a literary product of great mastery and marvel. Due to such an unpredictability of their work, contemporary biofiction authors share most of the premises of postmodern uncertainty, which calls for a closer look at postmodernity and postmodernism in particular.

Like any other previous socio-cultural and historical period, postmodernism also emerged as a reaction to the previous aesthetic ideal. Its emergence and development cannot be separated from the broader developments in the world. Postmodernism has followed the rise of new ideas, technologies and lifestyles in Europe and North America as a result of the rapid technological development in an ever-increasing globalization. According to Simon Malpas (2005), to be postmodern involves living on the fast track of exchanging ideas and experiences in transformed and annihilated borders of social interactions. Both the virtual and the physical mobility of people has added to the "shrinking of the world" and the immediate availability of information (Malpas 2005:1).

Such fluidity inevitably leads to the transformation of every aspect of living. People have become accustomed to having everything at the press of a button. Nothing seems to hold any mystery anymore. A person is no longer responsible to the immediate environment but has a direct impact across the same global world of economy and culture. This same world of globalization is the main instrument of letting postmodernity into people's lives.

It is evident that the contemporary way of life and work have brought about multiple worldviews that have challenged tradition and society. Postmodernism reflects those changes and tries to respond to all the challenges in the social, political and philosophical world. However contradictory in its essence, postmodernism can still be put within a certain framework of diverse sets of rules and characteristics. As a key term in contemporary studies in the humanities, postmodernism has been used by media and social science to describe the spirit of the time and the major developments in culture, philosophy and politics. As a result, postmodernism has been defined in respect to different areas and disciplines.

Some of the most important and most influential explanations of the postmodern thinking and its implications can be traced in such areas as identity, history, art, literature, culture and politics. Literary postmodernism, in particular, introduces challenging ways of transforming ideas. Being so widely applicable, it comprises a wide array of theoretical strands that both intersect and multiply in their definitions. Most significantly, literary postmodernism has come to represent the literary styles, modes and techniques that succeeded modernism in the second half of the twentieth century.

According to Linda Hutcheon (2003:19), postmodern authors aim to supersede previous theoretical preoccupations by denying and accepting them at the same time.

> In essence, the postmodern text is made of a range of strands not making a coherent whole but continuously contradicting each other. What postmodernism does, as its very name suggests, is confront and contest any modernist discarding or recuperating of the past in the name of the future.
> (Hutcheon 2003:19)

Due to the fact that the major technological and lifestyle changes have inevitably brought about thematic and formal changes in literature, postmodernism has introduced new ways of connecting art and life. Unlike modernist authors, postmodernists do not use framing as a literary technique, there is no hero's journey archetype, no effective use of flashbacks, no universal or common themes or character development, the role of the reader is not determined by the author and there is no stream of consciousness narration. Instead, very often postmodern authors reject past norms and deliberately turn to new fractured and fragmented forms of expression often to present as artistic something formerly seen as un-artistic. As Umberto Eco (1983) points out: "The postmodern reply to the modern consists of recognizing that the past, since it cannot really be destroyed, because it leads to silence, must be revisited: but with irony, not innocently."

In terms of depicting reality, postmodern literature has been directly connected to contemporary perceptions of culture, communication, information and disinformation. Modern technologies and means of communication dictate the placement and reception of information in the contemporary world. In this respect, news items and all other kinds of information are presented simultaneously across the media, all aiming to present the truth, to incorporate fiction where necessary and to become relevant. These developments have been inevitably infiltrated in literary creation turning postmodernist art into an art characterized by fragmentation and multiplicity of themes and voices. These postmodernist characteristics are one of the major reasons for the pervading plurality in contemporary literary creation.

Postmodernist authors use old literary forms, genres and types to re-contextualize their meanings and produce different cultural, linguistic and semiotic contexts. The creative potential of the postmodern work is in the production of new forms, styles and genres out of the existing ones by intentional borrowings from other sources. In terms of literature and novelistic writing, such use entails postmodern genre play. As Jaroslav Kušnír (2011) observes, it is in this way that a multiplicity of readings becomes possible and that the notions of auto/biography, for example, shift from an idea of presenting "the truth" about someone to portraying "a truth", or a cluster of "truths". Plurality and the constant borrowings entail the persistent presence of the past in the present and the future. On a textual level, the postmodern literary text resonates postmodern literary modes and techniques in all its segments. Postmodernist authors willingly incorporate different generic modes and techniques of writing in an incessant creative play while shaping their work.

It is a set view nowadays that some of the most important among those postmodernist generic modes and techniques of writing are the palimpsest, the collage, the pastiche, as well as intertextuality, metafiction and relativism (Kušnír 2011). One of the first to focus extensively on the significance of the palimpsest in postmodern writing is Gérard Genette in his book *Palimpsests* (1997) (first published in French as *Palimpsestes* (1982)) to be followed by others such as one of the more recent studies of the use of the palimpsest in postmodernism, Sarah Dillon's *The Palimpsest: Literature, Criticism, Theory* (2007). All these studies take up the original definition of the palimpsest as "a paper or parchment on which the original text has been partly erased or effaced to allow a new text to be written, leaving fragments of the original still visible" (Macey 2000:228) to define it in postmodern literature as the "rewriting of the old texts by putting them in different linguistic and cultural contexts" (Kušnír 2011:33).

Another technique that postmodern authors often use in the formal composition of the text is collage. It enables plurality, relativism and genre hybridity in the narrative. Like all other literary techniques, the postmodernist collage also has its specific characteristics. Kušnír sees the postmodernist collage as different from the modernist one, in the idea that the meaning of different styles, chapters, etc. in the modernist collage is visible in the connection with the other, while the elements or parts creating a postmodern collage in a literary work are mostly self-sufficient and can themselves create meaning of their own, although, of course, the full understanding of such a work requires reading of all parts, elements or segments of the text.

(Kušnír 2011:39)

The aspect of plurality and relativization of the postmodernist work requires that the postmodernist collage is shaped like that.

Almost inseparable from these two is the pastiche. According to Kušnír, pastiche means the use of different genres, styles, voices and techniques in the creation of a literary work. He claims that unlike the past when the practitioners of pastiche were criticized for uncreative and mechanical imitation of other works of art, in postmodernism, this word has come to signify something positive, "since the older works of art, styles and authors are first imitated but, at the same time, through the use of parody and irony further transformed, re-written and put in a different linguistic context" (Kušnír 2011:38). Nevertheless, Kušnír further claims that pastiche and parody can overlap as postmodernism refuses to follow strict definitions. Consequently, the use of such devices is often interdependent and interchangeable.

The use of these generic modes in postmodern writing is intrinsically connected to intertextuality, which expresses the connection between texts by using the devices and techniques of postmodernism in terms of mixture of genres and styles as well as direct application of pastiche, kitsch and parody. Nevertheless, intertextuality is not a single mechanical connection, but rather a creative transformation of the referred texts in different linguistic and cultural contexts. In Julia Kristeva's view (Kristeva 1980), a text is a mosaic of quotations, and it is absorption and transformation of another one. The stories exist in specific literary and cultural contexts, open to different interpretations. Parody, pastiche and irony form another aspect of postmodern literary works (Kušnír 2011:36).

Hutcheon makes a distinction between postmodernist parody and traditional parody. "Postmodernist parody, be it in architecture, literature, painting, film or music uses its historical memory, its aesthetic introversion, to signal that this kind of self-reflexive discourse is always inextricably bound to social discourse" (Hutcheon 2003:35). Unlike traditional parody, postmodern parody does not mock the parodied author or style for its own sake. For Hutcheon

(2003), postmodern parody lacks this mocking, ridiculing aspect and by adding irony it emphasizes a difference between the past forms of art and sensibilities, a distance between the past and the present. In this respect, parody and irony in postmodern literature are very closely connected or almost inseparable. Hutcheon emphasizes the subversive impulses of parody in regard to political and ideological aspects. "Postmodern parody is both deconstructively critical and constructively creative, paradoxically making us aware of both the limits and the powers of representation—in any medium" (Hutcheon 2003:94).

Hutcheon further argues that in the interest of precision and consistency, the self-conscious dimension of history has to be added to the definition of postmodern literature. In this sense, postmodernism brings together the discourse of art with the discourse of history. Historiographic metafiction works to contextualize past events in a specific creative process, resulting in a literary artifact.

Historiographic metafiction is closely connected to relativism which in postmodernism is expressed in the

> text's rejection of a close and clear ending in favor of the open ending in which a reader has space to participate in the creation of meaning of text: in offering multiple and relative rather than clear and unifying perspectives: in a constant evocation of doubt and self-evaluation of characters.
>
> (Kušnír 2011:33)

Such relativism leaves open the creation of reality. The reader is given an active role in evaluating and identifying stories, events and characters' actions.

In this respect, relativism is largely connected with the metafictional status of the postmodern work. By referring to its own metafictional status, the text becomes metafictional. According to Kušnír (2011), the metafictional work "refers to itself and the principles of its construction by using various techniques and narrative devices" (Kušnír 2011:33). He further argues that in addition to the general claim that "metafiction is fiction about fiction", metafiction, metafictional elements and metafictionality are integral parts of a postmodern literary work.

> By using metafictional elements, the postmodern authors point out a difference between reality and its linguistic representation

and they emphasize the fact that a language works on different principles than reality. At the same, the use of metafictional elements point[s] out the fictionality of fiction, involve a reader in a creation of meaning of the literary (artistic) text, and shows a difference between the past and contemporary forms of art, between the past and present sensibility and the vision of the world.

(Kušnír 2011:34)

Metafiction builds its status with the help of many of its elements such as quotation, allusion, false, fake quotation, paraphrasing, parody, pastiche, irony and intertextuality. In Kušnír's view, these devices are used to mark the "connection between the literary text a reader reads and other works of art, documents, historical records or theories" (Kušnír 2011:35).

All of these postmodern techniques and devices form an integral part in the postmodern genre play. They form and shape unique narratives while showing potential for myriads of meanings and textual formations.

As seen above, the concept of genre as a social action/event, as a textual interaction and a textual practice is predetermined to adopt and adapt itself to countless textual manifestations. As such, genres exhibit their potential for unique textual transformations which, in turn, entails generic transformation. As a result, genres always ensure a degree of playfulness as their intrinsic characteristic. The genre play that takes place in postmodern genre blending, therefore, establishes a specific textual realm. In life-writing genre play, in particular, this realm is governed by intricate narrative modes and techniques while combining the distinct notions of fact and fiction. When this play is part of the writing about the lives of famous historical figures, it always ends with a powerful social statement, a new reality or a thematization at the interface of the fact and fiction combination.

2 Auto/biography and literature

2.1 Literary biography

Interestingly, following the publication of *Biofictions: The Rewriting of Romantic Lives in Contemporary Fiction and Drama* by Martin Middeke and Werner Huber in 1999, it took almost twenty years for a surge of authorships on biofictions. As mentioned above, few books on biofictions appeared in the meantime following certain trends in biofictional bestselling writing, such as Madeleine Danova's *Jamesiad, The Postmodern Lives of Henry James* (2011). Probably, the peak started around 2017. In 2018, Richard Bradford published *A Companion to Literary Biography*. The book provides a comprehensive study of literary biography across three centuries pointing to the importance of literary criticism in that respect. Nora Goldsmith's *Afterlives of the Roman Poets: Biofiction and the Reception of Latin Poetry* in 2019 connects biofictional reception to the interpretation of the classics. The year of 2020 saw at least three important studies on biofictions: Bethany Layne's *Biofictions and Writers' Afterlives*, a collection of essays illustrating the portrayal of different writers in biofictions, *Neo-Victorian Biofictions: Reimagining Nineteenth Century Historical Subjects* edited by Marie Luise-Kohlke and Christian Gutleben explores the ethical consequences of combining biography and fiction. In 2022, Virginia Newhall Rademacher published *Derivative Lives, Uncertainty and Speculative Risk in Contemporary Spanish Narrative* delves on biofiction in Spain and globally, relating literary expression to concepts such as circumstantiality, derivatives, speculation and game studies. In his "Biofiction, Documentality and the Internet. Metmorphoses of a Literary Genre" (2015), Riccardo Castellana claims:

> To avoid confusion, I propose to make a clear distinction between *type a* fictional biographies, i.e. fiction in a biographical form about an unreal character like *Marbot* or in the

DOI: 10.4324/9781003327790-3

allodiegetic domain, like Nabokov's *The True Life of Sebastian Knight* and *type b* ficitional biographies i.e. biographies of real, historical characters but in fictional form (and in some cases, but not necessarily with fictional, invented episodes of minor characters).

(Castellana 2015:119)

This division is an interesting addition to the general discussion of the different types of biofictional genres, resulting from the life-writing genre play. The fact that the mentioned biofiction *Marbot* was published by Wolfgang Hildesheimer in 1981 further adds to a more detailed study of the specific genre play. Although not the central topic of concern, this was confirmed by Julia L. Abramson, in her "Translation as Metaphor in Hildesheimer's Marbot Eine Biographie" (1996) say:

> In Marbot's biography, the factual and the fictional are admixed to tease a reader's credulity and strain his erudition to the point that more than one prominent reader was deceived, for a time, into believing this novel to be factual historical biography.
>
> (Abramson 1996:104)

One of the first attempts to theorize literary biography was made by Michael Benton. Following the publication of his earlier book, *Literary Biography: An Introduction* (2009), in his 2015 book *Towards a Poetics of Literary Biography*, Benton proposes a series of frameworks for the genre's analysis. His underlining question is whether a theory of biography is even possible in a genre that necessarily is submerged in a historical narrative. At the same time, to complete such theory, it is necessary to use a wide range of concepts and approaches from other fields – from social studies, psychology, literary criticism, the law and moral philosophy (Benton 2015:x). Benton creates something that Moulin calls "comparative biography":

> [It is] an amply documented analytical survey of remarkable twentieth-century British biographies, with some excursions into the nineteenth century, especially to illustrate the notion of 'comparative biography', defined by Richard Holmes as examining the handling of one subject by a number of different biographers, and over different historical periods.
>
> (Moulin 2016)

In light of his comparative approach of different biographies dealing with the same person, Benton grounds his theory in the practice of the genre's creation. This is his starting point for examining the process of writing a literary biography. Next, he considers the contexts and meanings of the literary biographical texts and their effects in practice. This shows that, despite genre conventions, different biographers approach biographies differently at different times. As a result, it is practice, rather than theory that signals the complexity and the diversity of the genre. It is here that the poetics reveals the generic principles of the biographical form examining the effects achieved in the end.

Benton (2015) structures his study by considering the nature of the genre, that is, how a substantial body of data is dealt with in the biographical narrative. He then exemplifies this issue by looking into the historical and fictional aspects of biographical writing. He introduces matters concerning the biographer's presentation of literary figures and the issue of treating the biographee's own work in presenting their life.

Further in his study, Benton (2015) concludes that historical scholarship combined with literary flair is what lies at the heart of the poetics of literary biography, stressing some of the genre's particular principles in the formation of that poetics. These include ethical concerns, a sense of sympathy and an exercise of imagination.

A different approach is used by Michael Lackey whose study of the literary biography and its hybridized nature is integrated in the study of biofiction as a life-writing genre. Following the publication of his *Truthful Fiction: Conversations with American Biographical Novelists* (2014) and *The American Biographical Novel* (2016a), Michael Lackey's book, *Biographical Fiction. A Reader* (2016b) traces the origin and development of the twentieth- and twenty-first-century biographical novel featuring reflections of eminent authors and lecturers as well as interviews and essays from major critics.

The questions Lackey (2016b) poses regarding biofiction revolve around theories of knowledge and fiction that play a part in the creation of biofictions. Lackey's collection creates a bold contention when it comes to establishing the major ideas in life-writing genre blending. Looking at all the great biofictional novels that have been published over the last thirty years, Lackey suggests that this is the "golden age of biofiction". In his anthology, he has collected a wide variety of biofictional studies illustrating both primary and secondary sources.

The shift in the nature of literary truth and the meanings thus produced are also one of the main preoccupations of his previous book, *The American Biographical Novel* (2016a). According to Lackey (2016a), the "postmodern proliferation of truth systems" that has substituted the "one ultimate, absolute or dominant Truth that subsumes all other truths" is what leads to different symbolic representations in telling the life story of a person. Through the characters presented in the biographical novel, the authors manage to construct an image of their subject that stands for some idea in their time and place reflecting on the contemporary world at the same time. Some authors use the character structure rather than documentary evidence to construct the narrative. In this respect, he states, the readers should have in mind the author's interests in creating a literary symbol rather than the historical figure. As he claims in an interview with Rhys Tranter:

> Biographical novelists, who have actual historical figures as their protagonists hold that humans are so clearly and easily determined by external forces. To the contrary, they tend to foreground the degree to and the sense in which a resisting and active consciousness shapes and determines the social and political world.
>
> (Tranter 2016)

This claim is especially true for postmodern biofictional writing. The reliability of each documentary evidence is self-reflexively questioned. The result of such questioning is a possibility for a variety of interpretations each of which is equally plausible.

One concern regarding the theory and practice of biofiction is what the fictional techniques biographical novelists deploy and what they can achieve. According to Lackey (2016b), many contemporary writers choose to ground their work in history because of skepticism towards traditional literary symbols. While traditional fictional symbols can conveniently be constructed by the authors to serve their purpose and make a valid contribution to history, biographical novelists want to avoid the creation of arbitrary characters and resort to actual historical figures instead. Being novelists and not biographers they blend fact and fiction in inventing fictional scenes and characters. This understanding attests to some of the effects of postmodern fact and fiction binding. By using actual historical figures for their fictional plot lines, biofiction authors achieve a new level of expressing viewpoints and criticism.

This idea of fictionalization of biography has been in the focus of critical attention for quite some time. Georg Lukacs' 1937 "The Historical Novel" (Lackey 2016b:249–268) and Paul Murray Kendall's 1965 "The Art of Biography" (Lackey 2016b:275–283) show how biography and history are appropriated or "owned" in order to be "disowned" by fiction. Both the authors denounce these appropriations; Georg Lukacs defines the classical historical novel as a literary form that accurately presents political and economic forces, and gives the readers a precise picture of the essential factors influencing major social developments. Kendall defines the narrative form "in relation to life-writing". For him, "the novel-as-biography" is ultimately doomed to failure because it is almost wholly imaginary. In his understanding, the real-life picture of the past is replaced by a "wayward vision of wannabe novelists, thus disqualifying it as a legitimate biography" (Lackey 2016b:1).

Life-writing was the dominating intellectual influence throughout the whole period of the twentieth century as the collected essays in Lackey's *Reader* testifies. In most of the cases, scholars have foregrounded the biographical in the study of biofiction. Carl Bode's 1955 groundbreaking essay "The Buxom Biographies" (Lackey 2016b:269–274) disqualifies any writing as a biography if it is bad or stylized. Bode claims that biography stands for "unadorned truth" while an embellished truth makes the novel. Ina Schabert's "In Quest of the Other Person: Fiction as Biography" (Lackey 2016b:284–298) examines the ability of fictional biographies and biographical fictions to give readers knowledge of the real person. On the other hand, Alain Buisine's essay "Biofictions" from 1991 (Lackey 2016b:161–166) examines the genre of the biofiction as a new type of biography where an accurate presentation of the biographical subject is no longer possible because it has taken the form of fiction. More recently, Monica Latham's definition of biofiction from 2012 is that of a "hybrid narrative form that straddles two separate worlds, but ultimately suggests that the genre seeks to picture the biographical subject's 'life story', thus subordinating the fictional to the biographical" (Lackey 2016a:18). In contrast to these scholarly propositions, some of the authors of biofictions included in Lackey's *Reader* claim that they do not write biography or history but works of fiction. Such authors include Bruce Duffy, Joyce Carol Oates, Anne Enright, Jay Parini, Margaret Atwood,

Madison Smart Bell, Joanna Scott, Ilya Troyanov, Anita Diamant, Jerome Charyn, Hilary Mantel, David Lodge, Laurent Binet, Colm Toibin and David Ebershoft. Biofiction is distinct in how the genre play reworks the traits of either biography or fiction. The formal distinction is visible in the naming of the new form. Thomas Mallon (Lackey 2016b:60–63) states that word order and the subordination of the adjective and the noun when referring to something reveals the nature of the genre. When talking about writing historical fiction, an author writes fiction and not historiography or biography. He further claims that because of this word relation, it would be wrong to refer to biographical novels as fictionalized biographies and vice versa. Consequently, the word order can be considered as a valuable tool in determining the subgenres' distinct characteristics and make a difference between a biography, fictional biography and biographical fiction (Lackey 2016b:60–63).

Another example of the distinctions between these terms is Russell Banks' claim that he is really writing about a historical figure but strategically setting off his work from biography by writing a narrative employing dramatic shape and intent. Julia Alvarez also gives her reasons for genre distinction and discusses the wish of so many authors to call their work fiction rather than biography. According to her, the end result of portraying one's life lies in the author's talent, inclinations and abilities. Some are more inclined to become straight biographers, while others turn to different methods, approaches and objectives and thus write fiction (Lackey 2016b:203–216).

In examining the bio in biofiction and looking into the demands of the genre biography (representation) and fiction (creation) of the life story, the "fiction" is what modifies the "bio" in biofiction. Cora Kaplan's understanding that the "bio" in biofiction also refers to a more essentialized element of identity implies that there is something insoluble separating the two genres and preventing them from being invisibly stitched; in her understanding, the connection will always show (Kaplan 2007:65). Parini contrasts this idea by subordinating the biographical to the fictional. He claims that novels about lives and fiction have been made up with half believable discourse. In Parini's case, all accent is put on the author's vision (Lackey 2016a:22).

The cluster of illustrating the biographical and the fictional in the genre may be best summarized by Lackey's claim that the biographical novelists differ from biographers because, while authors of traditional and factual biographies seek to represent the life (or a dimension of a life) of an actual historical figure as clearly and accurately as possible, biographical novelists forego the desire to get the "biographical subject's life 'right' and rather use the biographical subject in order to protect their own vision of life and the world" (Lackey 2016a:22).

Overall, in most of his publications, in trying to define the distinctive characteristics of biographical fiction, Lackey defines what he calls "literary symbolism". While past authors altered the names of their protagonists based on real persons and gave them fictional names creating literary symbols, authors of biographical fiction do this by using the real name of the real-life protagonist making the literary symbol more emphatic. One of the reasons for the rise of the need for a "historically specific and empirically based literary symbol" is the postmodern claim that all systems of knowledge are limited, flawed and untrustworthy. When it comes to the protagonists of the biographical novels who are then turned into literary symbols, Lackey claims that the "historical-social type" of characters Lukacs talks about are different from the protagonists of the biographical novel because instead of being invented to function as symbols, the biofictional protagonists are idealized by their authors and do not represent the struggles and tensions of the historical-social type (Lackey 2016a:89). In this study, this principle is visible in the creation of the female literary symbols represented by Fitzgerald's wife Zelda and Hemingway's wives Hadley, Pauline, Martha and Mary. I call them primary literary symbols born out of the way their husband's story is told. Fitzgerald and Hemingway, on the other hand, get the position of subsidiary or secondary literary symbols.

My understanding, therefore, is very much in line with Lackey's answer to Lukacs' claim that the biographical novel cannot answer major questions because of its exaggerated and often embarrassing characters. He says that the biographical novel can "invert the historical novel" and offer a "new way of thinking about some historical moments", giving examples from Olsen's *Nietzsche's Kisses*. Thus, Lackey touches upon the hybridized form of biofiction convincingly illustrating the differences between biographical fiction and life-writing and the relation between fact and fiction. He claims that the authors of biofiction and life-writing make a different contract than biographers and historians of not altering the truth and representing their subject's life as accurately as possible. The biographer may have a biased ideological approach but that differs from a "purposeful and strategic alteration of fact" (Lackey 2016b:9). What they do, in fact, is to make a connection between the time of their subject's life and their own time in order to strategically convey bi-temporal truths. What is more, as Lackey believes, that turns them into literary symbols.

Further discussion is developed by Marcel Schwob. In the preface of his *Imaginary Lives* (1924), he points to the uniqueness of every living being and the necessity to address that in recounting a person's life. "The science of history leaves us uncertain as to individuals revealing only those points by which individuals have been attached to generalities. [...]Contrary to history, art describes individuals, desires only the unique. It does not classify, it unclassifies" (Schwob 1924 Preface: 7). He further proposes that biography can thus be considered art and as such:

> As an art, biography is founded upon choice; truth need not be its preoccupation, for out of a chaos of human traits it can create [...] In the midst of these great collections art must choose what it needs to compose a form that will be like no other form.
>
> (Schwob 1924:20)

Enhanced by the postmodernist and hypermodernist worldviews, this may be considered as a predecessor to the proliferation of genre blending towards the end of the twentieth century and the beginning of the twenty-first century.

This transformation is a clear illustration of how fact and fiction combine in biofictional writing. Furthermore, the purpose of the author in turning a person or event into a literary symbol is made possible by the metafictional nature of the genre. The metafictionality further confirms that biofictions do open the possibility of multiple truths and the plurality of meanings. That is one of the analytical focuses of the present study of Fitzgerald's and Hemingway's biofictions.

As noted above, before beginning his work, the literary biographer sets a clear goal, that of concocting a writer's biographical story. He becomes the genre's "puppet master". He recognizes the commonalities between the genres and how the genre play can masterfully counterfeit important story elements. Yet, he seems to approach his task earnestly and anxiously.

In this respect, the task of the biographer is very complex. His success depends on the creative design of the stories.

Unlike their counterparts in political and military fields, they sail in uniquely dangerous waters. To one side they face the hard rocks of historical data which they ignore at their peril; to the other, a whirlpool of imaginative literature which, for biographical purposes, is of uncertain depth and relevance.

(Benton 2009:265)

The literary biographer has multiple focal strands to deal with: the biographee's life material, their existing image in the world and the bibliography of previously published biographies. All of these starting points lead to ways that may intersect with or drift apart from the construction of the biofiction. The metafictional self-reflexivity is inevitable in this process.

Literary biography as a postmodern literary structure combines document facts with strong narrative impulse. It is a narrative product that inclines and declines from its historical necessities and its narrative characteristics leaving open the question of biographical 'truth'. Narrative, in other words is a discourse that may be generated in history or fiction – even in the blending of the two genres – in which the crucial element is the time. Literary biographies comprise life histories that are, by definition, incomplete and open to discussion. This put the authors of the literary biography in an ambivalent position. They are charged with the responsibility to present and account for the spectrum of the life from cradle to grave, yet equally expected to give point, significance and interest to that life through narrative modes of representation which are often more readily associated with fiction and which, in the biographer's interpolations and gap-filling, are constantly edging in that direction. In the writing process, the literary biographer is continuously moving between a conception of events that have occurred 'prior to entextualisation' and their representation as created by and with the text.

(Benton 2009:18)

The role of the literary biographer is two-fold then. He is compelled to impose his own understanding of the biographee's life while being constrained by credulity of the available facts and details at the same time. In this way, the literary biographer constantly shifts focus and perspective in compiling the story. The reason for this is the deconstruction of a certain life event, the certainty or uncertainty of it, its completeness or incompleteness. The literary biographer is set to create a life narrative that can often take the form of an experiment. He has to take the available material and shape its arbitrariness into an engaging text.

Moreover, data items can be marginalized, extended or expanded in biopreservation sequences by creating shorter or longer narrative inserts in the portrayal of the biographee's life. This view is in line with Lucasta Miller's idea about a biographer's creative work.

> Literary biography will continue to raise questions which need to be answered again and again – about the relationship between fact and truth, and between information and interpretation, as well as about the nature of personality and the relationship between writers and their writings. We should not see biography as a failed empirical science striving to produce definitive, objective results but doomed to failure. Nor should we take the extreme post-modernist line which completely collapses the distinction between biography and fiction, regarding both as undifferentiated 'textual constructs'. Instead, we should regard it as an amphibious art form, which ideally has both to obey the constraints of evidence and to respond creatively to the challenge of making shape, form and meaning.
>
> (Benton 2009:34)

Literary biographers then, have to be both "obeying the constraints of evidence" and "respond creatively to them", which entails the process of biopreservation and the creation of biopreservational sequences.

Biopreservation as a unique property of the biofictions allows for highly diverse narratives in scope and in character. Depending on the recurring biopreservation sequences, biofictions can lean into different image-making directions. The image-making in the end is supposed to interpret and confirm the ideas behind the biopreservation sequences.

Michael Lackey's most recent book, *Bioficton. An Introduction* (2021), gives a historical account of the origin and the rise of the genre of biofiction, the literary debates of the genre and its implication in a wider social, cultural and political context. While the book provides a comprehensive review of the developments surrounding biofictions, my book's approach goes in a different direction, i.e. it provides a literary theory on biofiction textuality.

2.2 Biopreservation: the building block of postmodern literary biography

In order to see what these narratives do and how they do it, it is necessary to explain some of the newly emerging terminology. As noted above, the advent of the genre brought on a number of terms associated with it, but all bearing on different theoretical fields. Conveniently, they all may fall under the umbrella of biofictional life-writing investigation.

> In such texts, historical data about a person who once lived are used explicitly in order to construct that person as a character in a work of fiction. Such works often overtly thematize the traditional distinction between the factual and the fictional. This type of writing has been classified variously as "fictional biography", "biofiction", "fictional metabiography", "the biographical novel" and "biographical fiction".
> (Viljoen 2013:155)

Biofictions deliberately move away from the standard notions of auto/biography in their attempt to procure specific image of the biographee. Moreover, their attempt is to achieve a particular sensibility through the narration and thereby distance from the standard biographical accounts. This is where the success of the genre lies, in the artistic skills of the author to organize and position the narrative in a clear direction. The biofiction author, by definition, enters the seemingly chaotic space of "fact and fiction" dichotomies in the attempt to offer their own solutions.

My argument is that this creative realm bears on the narrative elements as discussed by Herman, the narrative identity according to Dan P. McAdams and Genette's concept on textuality. These theoretical backgrounds simultaneously question and determine the narrative's frontiers. Such positioned framework allows for the analysis of the multiple genre blending in the biofictions about Fitzgerald and Hemingway. It fits the need for explaining and understanding the building of the narrative and the biopreservation sequences. In this respect, my analysis follows the pattern of uncovering the sequences, the narrative identity and its delicate shaping.

The proposed framework closely follows the progress of discussion. The main attributes assigned to it entail a more "rigorous" concept since they specifically apply to the genre of life-writing.

Here, the "self" and the narrative identity are more closely explored in light of the metafictional autobiographical writing. In particular, the study is devoted to making a connection between the narrative elements and their double origin as both fictional and factual and the building of Zelda and Hadley's fictional narrative identities. For that purpose, I develop the analytical approach of the biopreservation sequences. It fulfills the goal of establishing biopreservation as a type of textuality concerning life-writing. As such, it is enabled by the specific interplay between fact and fiction. Notwithstanding, it is necessary to make the analysis in order to illustrate and apply the concept's arguments. In this way, my reasoning can be considered complete and open for further discussion.

To verify all that, I make the necessary revisions, looking for any possible counterarguments. This study's multiple life-writing illustration is chosen to suffice both the length and the quality of the discussion. To that end, the specific textuality behind the narrative elements is always kept in perspective while uncovering the intricate life-writing genre play. In this sense, according to Nünning:

> this crossing of traditional genre boundaries is not confined to a blurring of the fact and fiction boundary, but extends to hybrid new forms of biofiction. [...], this blurring of genre conventions has resulted in the emergence of such new generic variants of the fictional biography (which is in itself a hybrid form) as the revisionist fictional biography, the fictional metabiography and the fictional metaautobiography.
> (Nünning 2005:199)

Hence, the two biofictions about Zelda and Hadley exhibit a peculiar narrative. The first-person fictional narrators of Zelda and Hadley use the facts from the women's real counterparts' lives in order to set the meaning, the structure and the background of their life stories. In addition, the comparison of those two works with the biofiction written in the first person by the fictional acquaintance of Hemingway and the two autobiographical and memoirist accounts by the real wives of Fitzgerald and Hemingway further uncovers the dominating idea of the genre play and the ensuing textual characteristics.

The titles of the primary biofictions of discussion are the most obvious indicators of a "full" genre play. The word "novel" in the title *Z: A Novel of Zelda Fitzgerald* marks the genre as fictional, only subtly suggesting that it might be about Zelda's life in that her name and surname are the same as those of a real historical person. The title of McLain's biofiction entails double generic meaning as anybody could be a "Paris wife". The "contractual" rule of Lejeune for the three-part pact is thus breached at the very beginning. According to Lejeune, the "real author, narrator and the title page coincide and seek to interpret their own life" (Saunders 2010:4).

The perceived differences arise from the general conventions of the auto/biographical and metafictional genres and the immediacy of their concomitant characteristics is automatically called into question. As Nünning (2005) observes:

> Metabiographies and metaautobiographies serve to foreground the main characteristics of the two genres in question, while also showing that these conventions are elements of the collective memory (shared by authors and readers alike) crystallized in schemata and that they guide the interpretative strategies and expectations along certain paths.
>
> (Nünning 2005:209)

From here on, the complexity increases, but not without a common ground which in this case is auto/biography. Discussing life-writing and the place of autobiography as one form of life-writing, Saunders (2010) rightfully contends that:

> We need the term to hold the varieties of life-writing forms together because individual works tend to combine them anyway, and readers can move across the generic borders as writers can. Our postmodern way of thinking about biography is much more aware of, and open to these elements of autobiography and fiction in all life-writing. Such generic blurring is characteristic in another way. Life-writing is fundamentally intertextual. Biographies quote freely from their subject's letters or diaries or speeches where available. Memoirists quote conversation they claim to remember verbatim. One might think autobiography would provide generic purity, relying on acts of memory for its sources. Yet, autobiographers, too, quote documents, other biographies, their own journals and novels, though by the same principles of generic fusion such sources will themselves be already fused.
>
> (Saunders 2010:5–6)

Consequently,

> These terms "autobiografiction" and "autofiction" are comparably double-joined, indicating that auto/biography can be read as fiction and that fiction can be read as auto/biographical.
>
> (Saunders 2010:7)

In this sense, Saunders (2010) lists different patterns of auto/biographical fictions, illustrating the numerous possibilities of the roman à clef.

The case of the biofictions subject to this study goes one step further from the above concept on the auto/biographical conventions. Their status as fictional auto/biographies written about the lives of real persons involves the presence of metafiction and the quest of the self. "Like its autobiographical counterpart, the fictional metabiography constitutes a particularly interesting species of generic self-reflexivity, one that critically explores the generic conventions and memory of the genre to which it belongs viz. the art of biography or life-writing" (Nünning 2005:209).

In line with this claim is Helga Schwalm's view on the current state of life-writing and autobiography:

> The field of life-writing as narratives of self—or of various forms of self—has thus become significantly broader, transcending the classic model of autobiographical identity qua coherent retrospective narrative. Yet whatever its theoretical remodeling and practical rewritings, even if frequently subverted in practice, the close nexus between narrative, self/identity, and the genre/practice of autobiography continues to be considered paramount. The underlying assumption concerning autobiography is that of a close, even inextricable connection between narrative and identity, with autobiography the prime generic site of enactment.
>
> (Schwalm 2014)

In this sense, the quest of the self, presented through an auto/biographical narrative is shaped by the narrative identity and in this case by the fictional autobiographical narrators of Zelda and Hadley. The analysis of their narrators shows how successful their appropriation was, by looking into the "stability" of the narrative identities they establish. The "stability" inevitably touches upon the "probability" of the autobiographical truth since "autobiographical truth is not a fixed but an evolving content in an intricate process of self-discovery and self-creation and further, that the self that is in the center of all autobiographical narratives is necessarily a fictive structure" (Eakin 1985:3).

Furthermore, the postmodernist overtones of such narratives could indicate any possible changes in ontological principles, decorum and appropriation. Metafiction, however, is unobtrusive in the biofictions subject to this study.

When it comes to the fictional autobiographies, the situation is quite particular. The fictional narrators impersonate the autobiographical subjectivity of their biographees by embracing the notions of memory, experience, identity, space, creation and object. These postulates of autobiographical writing are the essential material for illuminating the different stages of the narrative identity.

The fictional autobiographical accounts of Zelda and Hadley are also set to produce a fictional account whose allegiance to truth is not only nominal but aims to achieve high probability. Through their narrative identities both fictional Zelda and fictional Hadley purport to account for the initially unaccountable. McAdams's and Kate McLean's (2013) narrative identity elements of *redemption, communion, agency, contamination, coherent positive resolution, exploratory narrative processing* and *meaning-making* secure the person's understanding, development and adaptation to the living circumstances. Considering such coding, and the broader parameters of telling a story, one can examine the personal narratives about one's life.

The fictional autobiographical identities of Zelda and Hadley do not fall under the ordinary pattern of narrative identity formation since they are mediated through the creative wisdom of the biofiction authors. Their identity is operated by a specific type of textuality, the one I termed biopreservation. It is a specific type of textuality or even an intertextual subtype belonging to the art of life-writing.

The biofiction authors build their fictional narratives by entering their characters' inner worlds and making these worlds into a story according to the chronological events in their biographees' lives. The specificity of their identity lies precisely in how the events are interpreted and shaped as settings, causes, reasons and consequences. In this respect, Herman's theory about the narrative elements is important because it shows the deliberate arrangement of the events but does not show how that is done. Biopreservation, then, provides the answer for all the challenges on a storytelling level. It determines the characters' beliefs and ideas, and therefore, establishes the narrative identity. It further underlines how the narrative identity responds to the different actions or dramatic events.

The analysis will determine whether or not Fowler and McLain conquered the obstacles of being "surrogates" in representing Zelda and Hadley's selves and how biopreservation accounts for the "true-to-life" presentation of the biographees' lives. To this end, the analysis closely inspects the structure of the narratives looking for the narrative elements, their biopreservation properties and the ensuing thematic coding of the narrative identity.

Zelda and Hadley variously shuffle between recovery, sacrifice, growth and learning, betrayal, loss, failure, illness/injury, achievement/responsibility, empowerment, self-exploration, positive resolutions and understanding. Following that, we can see how the inner understanding of the fictional Zelda and Handley evolves in its certainty, firmness and determination.

This, as well as the structural coherence of the narrative, is revealed as I uncover the narrative elements. The elements predetermine the temporal, causal and thematic coherence of the narrative. They are composed of biopreservation sequences as the smallest constitutive part of the element. Thus shaped, the narrative affects the narrator's sense of the self, turning it into one or more thematic elements, finally establishing the complete idea of the identity.

These findings serve to prove and validate the particularities of the genre-blending textuality in life-writing as well as the overall structure of the narrative.

3 F. Scott Fitzgerald and Ernest Hemingway as fictional characters

Before I begin the critical analysis, it is necessary to make an overview of the other biofictions written about F. Scott Fitzgerald and Ernest Hemingway.

3.1 Fictionalizing Hemingway

According to one of the most recent studies on that topic, McFarland's 2014 *Appropriating Hemingway: Using Him as a Fictional Character*, Hemingway has become a fictional character in more than thirty novels, several short stories, graphic novels, plays and poems. In organizing his work, McFarland presents texts (mostly novels) in which Hemingway acquires considerable attention as a character as opposed to those in which he makes only cameo appearance. The large number of texts appropriating Hemingway as a fictional character includes those which present him either as a protagonist or as perceived through an obsessed character who is not always "favorably" minded. McFarland enumerates six novels concerned with 1920s Paris featuring Hemingway prominently: Vincent Cosgrove's *The Hemingway Papers* (1983), Howard Engel's *Murder in Montparnasse* (1992), Tony Hays' *Murder in the Latin Quarter* (1993), Clancy Carlile's *The Paris Pilgrims* (1999), Craig McDonald's *One True Sentence* (2011) and Paula McLain's *The Paris Wife* (2011). In addition to this list, there are several novels in which Hemingway's figure is portrayed as seen by an obsessed character as in Michael Palin's *Hemingway's Chair* (1995). In Gerhard Köpf's *Papa's Suitcase* (1994), Hemingway is idolized, at least by the protagonist, who may himself be treated at times as a bit of a buffoon, while Karl Alexander's *Papa and Fidel* (1989) and Dan Simmons' *The Crook Factory* (2000) feature Hemingway as an action-hero. Writers of mysteries and crime novels appear

DOI: 10.4324/9781003327790-4

to have been especially drawn to Hemingway, often to assist their protagonist or to behave as a sort of foil (McFarland 2014:25–55).

As seen above, Hemingway's appropriation as a character in biographical fictions varies widely. In most of the books mentioned above, his fictional character is the hero, but in a few of them he fails to become one. There is a group of books, however, in which Hemingway is represented in such a pejorative way that their authors can rightly be called "fanemies" as McFarland (2014:149) suggests. One such example is Marty Beckerman's satire, very tellingly entitled *The Heming Way: How to Unleash the Booze-Inhaling, Animal-Slaughtering, War-Glorifying, Hairy-Chested Retro-Sexual Legend Within, Just Like Papa!* (2012). Hemingway's image acquires even greater diversity in the so-called "speculative" fictions such as Joe Haldeman's *Hemingway Hoax* (1990), Tom Winton's *Hemingway's Ghost* (2011) and Craig McDonald's *Print the Legend* (2010). In these books, Hemingway is given unrealistic characteristics, often to achieve a comical effect.

Another group of biographical fictions about Hemingway are those in which he appears indirectly or as seen by the others. The influence his image has on the rest of the characters is often vital for their actions or the development of the story. Such novels include Bill Granger's *Hemingway's Notebook* (1986) and Edmundo Desnoes' *Memories of Underdevelopment* (2004).

Most recently, in 2018, another non-fiction work was published dealing with a rather neglected aspect of Hemingway's life, i.e. his meeting of the young Adriana Ivanchich in 1948 in Venice. The book is called *Autumn in Venice (Hemingway's Last Muse)* written by Andrea DiRobilant. The book portrays the special relationship between Hemingway and Adriana as crucial for the author's personal and professional well-being during the last decade of his life.

What this study tries to show is that the image Hemingway created of himself during his lifetime continues to be re-created today. In an attempt to understand this global development in the literary, cultural and everyday life of people, McFarland offers the concepts of "fandom" and "pop fiction". He insists that because the author's works can hardly be separated from their personal life stories, people who become fans of a story, a character or an idea, idolize the whole concept and work towards the creation of a particular public image. The aspect of fandom or of "how we make sense of the world, in relation to mass media, and in relation to our historical, social, cultural location" (McFarland 2014:11), is closely related to the rising popularity of biographical fiction, which gives ground to classifying it as a pop fiction. For McFarland, it can also fall into the realm of popular reading, to the world of escapist and formulaic fiction, of detective or spy novels, thrillers and pulp fiction, and, of course, "best sellers". The Modern Language Association lists more than 4,400 publications such as books, articles, thesis and dissertations dealing with the life and works of Hemingway. Many biographies and collections of letters have been published and new collections continue to be published. For example, the works published by Hemingway's friend A. E. Hotchner shortly after Hemingway's death continue to spawn biofictions today, probably because of the strong bond that was created by the writer and his "fan" and friend. As McFarland explains:

> Hemingway was nearly fifty when he met Ed Hotchner ('Hotch,' as he often called him), who was born in St. Louis in 1920, graduated from Washington University Law School in 1941, and served as a military journalist in the Air Force during World War II. Hotchner adapted several of Hemingway's works for the stage and television, and he later developed a close friendship with the actor Paul Newman. In his foreword, Hotchner celebrates Hemingway's 'courageous exploits' but draws attention to his 'shy and gentle' side and to his boundless generosity, 'charismatic personality,' and 'genius for friendship.' But he does observe that 'Ernest's standards of friendship were very high and difficult to define' and that he demanded those friends to 'measure up,' that they be 'straight and unphony and formed in their own image.'
>
> (McFarland 2014:21)

I agree that the author and the reader of a biographical fiction would most probably be "the faithful fans" of the famous protagonists, but I also believe that the idea of creating a new image or re-confirming an old idea about the lives of these figures is what triggers the wish to write or read biofiction. This is, in fact, the major focus of my analysis, since for me it offers the best manifestation of the process I have called "biopreservation".

In this sense, Hemingway's appropriations as a fictional character can be seen as having many purposes. They either resolve, praise or criticize his public or private figure. Such appropriations include presentation or re-representation of Hemingway not only as America's modern idol, a "clumsy womanizing drunk" or a charismatic man of sports and courage but also the opposite of these traits. For example, the books I analyze, Paula McLain's *The Paris Wife*, Erika Robuck's *Hemingway's Girl* and Martha Gellhorn's *Travel's with Myself and Another* give a different perspective of not only Hemingway's life and work but also of his wives' lives. Working at "preserving" certain parts of his life and discarding others, both McLain and Robuck have accessed a large body of biographies and documents about Ernest Hemingway's life and especially about Hadley Richardson Hemingway. First, there is Hemingway's memoir *A Moveable Feast* (1964), in which he makes a special tribute to Hadley, then interviews of her by Denis Brian for *The True Gen* (1988) and Berenice Kert's *The Hemingway Women* (1983). There are also the two biographies about Hadley: Alice Hunt Sokoloff's *Hadley: The First Mrs. Hemingway* (1971) and Gioia Diliberto's *Paris without End: The True Story of Hemingway's First Wife* (1992, 2011) as well as the *Cambridge Edition of the Letters of Ernest Hemingway (Book 1)* published in September 2011.

My primary goal is to see the way biopreservation works as it is expressed in these distinctly different narratives: a story about Hemingway fictionally told by his first wife Hadley Richardson, a story told by his third wife Martha Gellhorn in her own memoir as well as a story told by a fictional female character of Hemingway's servant during his second marriage to Pauline. I am not analyzing the more recent publication *Mrs. Hemingway* (2014) by Naomi Woods in which Hemingway's life is presented through the eyes of all four of his wives, because it would not add much to the discussion of my particular topic – genre play. My other reason for the choice I have made is that Hemingway's first two wives unlike Martha Gellhorn and Mary Welsh did not pursue writing careers despite Pauline's journalistic career, and therefore, there are no first-person biographical accounts of their life with Hemingway. The only biography about Pauline revealing an unseen side of her, *Unbelievable Happiness and Final Sorrow: The Hemingway-Pfeiffer Marriage* by Ruth Hawkins, was published considerably late, in 2012. I have chosen Gellhorn's story rather than that of Hemingway's last wife Mary Welsh presented in her book *How It Was* (1976) because of its more postmodernist approach to dealing with fact and fiction. According to many critics, Welsh's book, on the other hand, has a more realistic approach in portraying her life with Hemingway. As a result, while taking on a unique genre play interweaving fact and fiction, the three biofictional stories told by the three female characters both question and confirm "a truth" about their characters' lives and are a very good example of how the process of biopreservation works as the analysis to follow reveals.

3.2 Fictionalizing Fitzgerald

Similar to Hemingway's appropriation as a fictional character is that of F. Scott Fitzgerald and his wife Zelda Fitzgerald. Numerous biographies, collection of letters and biographical fictions have appeared about their lives, too. The list of such works is long and diverse. Many of them fall into the group of literary biographies about F. Scott Fitzgerald that Joyce Carol Oates designates as "pathographies" (Kakutani 1999), i.e. emphasizing the vice, evil or illness of the author.

The existing documentation about the Fitzgeralds is essential in the creation of their biographies. The first substantial publishing of their letters was made by Matthew J. Bruccoli in *F. Scott Fitzgerald: A Life in Letters* (1994) and in *The Collected Works of Zelda Fitzgerald* (1992). In 2002, the first collection of Scott and Zelda's letters in one volume *Dear Scott, Dearest Zelda: The Love Letters of F. Scott and Zelda Fitzgerald* was published by Jackson R. Bryer and Cathy W. Barks.

Lists of novels trying to uncover the enigmatic parts of their lives continuously spring up. In 2013 alone, six biographical fictions were released about Scott and Zelda Fitzgerald. Therese Ann Fowler's *Z: A Novel of Zelda Fitzgerald*, Erika Robuck's *Call Me Zelda* and R. Clifton Spargo's *Beautiful Fools: The Last Affair of Zelda and Scott Fitzgerald* feature Zelda as one of the main characters. In *Careless People: Murder, Mayhem and the Invention of Great Gatsby* by Sarah Churchwell, *Guests on Earth: A Novel* by Lee Smith and *Flappers: Six Women of a Dangerous Generation* by Judith Mackrell, her life story is presented alongside other people's life stories and plot lines. The novels take on the task of revising the treatment of Scott and Zelda as public figures while addressing the established facts in their standard biographies. In *Z: A Novel of Zelda Fitzgerald*, Therese Ann Fowler writes about what Fischer calls "Zelda's self-help epiphanies" (Fischer 2013). It is about "Zelda's grand romance and its ugly conflicts as well as the hopeful suggestion of Zelda's emergence as a self-actualized woman" (Fischer 2013).

In *Call Me Zelda*, Robuck introduces the character of Anna, a nurse in a Baltimore psychiatric hospital who befriends Zelda and the two manage to help each other go through difficult periods in their lives. Both Zelda and Anna adopt the language of therapy to alleviate and cure their pain. Anna tells Zelda's stories based on what Zelda writes and while helping Zelda, she finds a friend to whom she can confess all her troubles (a dead husband and a child, abandoned musical pursuits). Anna continues to tend to Zelda even after she leaves the hospital while also joining the Fitzgeralds on a trip to Bermuda, eventually becoming Zelda's true friend.

Spargo's *Beautiful Fools* tells a story of the last trip of the couple to Cuba which is the last trip they take together and the last time they see each other. The story uses local scenes and characters, including a Cuban playboy, a night club stabbing and an aged fortune teller. The story encompasses one of the less known stories about the couple's life and this makes it considerably more successful as a biographical fiction. Churchwell's *Careless People: Murder, Mayhem and the Invention of Great Gatsby* traces the couple's life story at the very beginning of their marriage in America. Their stay in New York at that time coincided with some bizarre crime events in the autumn of 1922 involving a double murder in New Jersey. These developments eventually inspired the conception of Fitzgerald's *The Great Gatsby*. *Guest's on Earth: A Novel* and *Flappers: Six Women of a Dangerous Generation* portray Zelda alongside other people's stories. The former deals with the events taking place in 1936 in Highland Hospital in Ashville, North Carolina. A thirteen-year-old orphaned Evalina Toussaint admitted to this institution is under Zelda's protection. She witnesses a number of events including the 1948 tragic fire killing nine women in a lock ward, one of which is Zelda. The latter tells the stories of six notable women of the Jazz Age their struggles and triumphs. These stories, including that of Zelda, are often intertwined and compared giving a richer perspective of the times and the people of the period.

Another group of fictional appropriations, just as is the case with those of Hemingway's life, casts the Fitzgeralds as secondary characters. *Gatsby's Girl* (2006) by Caroline Preston traces the life of Scott's first love, Ginevra. From their first meeting to her marital life, the book concentrates on her happy and sad moments. *Villa America* (2015) by Liza Klaussmann is another story about love and marriage in the Jazz age ex-pat community of young Americans in France. The golden age of the main protagonists Sarah and Gerald Murphy sadly does not last. The story features the Fitzgeralds, Hemingway, Picasso, Dos Passos and many other writers and artists attending the parties at the French Riviera. Prior to that, the life of the Murphy family was classically portrayed in *Living Well Is the Best Revenge* (1971) by Calvin Tomkins. A. Scott Borg's *Maxwell Perkins: Editor of Genius* (1978) is a book about the life of Maxwell Perkins, the editor of Fitzgerald, Hemingway's and Thomas Wolfe's work. He plays a crucial role in the authors' lives and careers dealing with all their personal and professional struggles.

Furthermore, Scott's last years in Hollywood and his love affair with the columnist Sheila Graham are presented in Sheila's own autobiographical novel *Beloved Infidel* (1958) and in *Intimate Lies: F. Scott Fitzgerald and Sheila Graham: Her Son's Story* (1995) by Robert T. Westbrook. Stewart O'Nan's *West of Sunset* (2015) is another biographical fiction about that period of Fitzgerald's life. It is a story told by a third-person narrator, set in Hollywood intensely portraying Fitzgerald's last years during the glamorous Golden Years of Hollywood. The story delivers Fitzgerald's inner portrait, his thoughts and emotions. The book encloses an episode of his love affair with Sheila Graham and ends with his death and his imagined last thoughts before he dies.

All these novels show a very specific process of sieving through the fact and fiction of Scott and Zelda Fitzgerald's lives and trying to preserve what appears important to the writers. In most of the cases, it is a process based on existing factual accounts of their lives. It is interesting that the first lengthy biography of either of the two is about Zelda Fitzgerald, published by Nancy Milford in 1970, called *Zelda: A Biography*. A year later, another memoir was published by Zelda's friend Sara Mayfield called *Exiles from Paradise: Zelda and Scott Fitzgerald*. These books made the definitive biographies about the couple's lives trying to present a balanced approach in not taking sides with any of the two.

In 1991, two decades after the publication of Mayfield's book, another biography about Zelda Fitzgerald was published, Koula Svokos Hartnett's *Zelda Fitzgerald and the Failure of the American Dream for Women*, as the first biography to try to prove that Zelda's misdiagnosis as a mental patient was the result of a doctor's mistaken judgment. A decade later, other two biographies about Zelda were published aiming at distinguishing reality from legend. These include Kendall Taylor's *Sometimes Madness Is Wisdom, Zelda and Scott Fitzgerald: A Marriage* (2001) and *Zelda Fitzgerald: Her Voice in Paradise* (2002) and its second edition entitled *Zelda Fitzgerald, The Tragic, Meticulously Researched Biography of the Jazz Age High Priestess* (2011) by Sally Cline. These two biographies entirely concentrate on Zelda's position in her life and marriage. In 2004, another biography of Zelda, *Zelda Sayre Fitzgerald: An American Woman's Life* by Linda Wagner Martin, was published. Here, Zelda's central place as a cultural figure helps to reappraise the cultural milieu of the times as well as the role of women in twentieth-century America.

The same year as Mayfield's biography, 1971, a biography of Fitzgerald was also published, called *Crazy Sundays: F. Scott Fitzgerald in Hollywood* (1971) by Aaron Latham. The book offers a detailed account of Fitzgerald's life especially of his last years, although, due to some fictional elements, it is not considered a standard biography. Ten years later, Matthew J. Bruccoli published Fitzgerald's standard biography *Some Sort of Epic Grandeur* (1981).

In 2007, the first biographical fiction dealing primarily with the Fitzgeralds' marital life called *Alabama Song* was published in French by Gilles Leroy. The same year the book won the highest literary award in France, Prix Goncourt. This seems to have led to the subsequent avalanche of biofictions about Fitzgerald.

Out of all that long list of biofictions about the Fitzgeralds, I have chosen Therese Ann Fowler's *Z: A Novel of Zelda Fitzgerald* and Zelda's own book *Save Me the Waltz* since my primary interest lies in the revisions of the "grand narratives" of the lives of the two most popular American writers of the twentieth century. Moreover, *Z: A Novel of Zelda Fitzgerald* is one of the most acclaimed biofictions about this iconic family and it is the only one written in first person. Comparing it to Zelda's own fictionalized autobiography allows me to trace the process of biopreservation and to analyze the interplay of fact and fiction in postmodern writing as expressed in the generic characteristics of the works in the same way I do in the case of the works dealing with Hemingway that I have opted to analyze here.

On the other hand, the very titles *Z: A Novel of Zelda Fitzgerald* and *The Paris Wife* are quite suggestive of the fact that these works deal with more than just a biographical account of a person. That allows me to look into the main traits characterizing the newly emerged genre types and the ways of creating them. The first one, explicitly foregrounding the idea of the fictional, is a novel about Zelda and not a biography of her, while the second excludes any reference to a particular historical or individual figure, replacing them with a type – the life of a member of a well-known ex-patriate community. Furthermore, the two primary biofictions allow me to make a comparison between them as a newly formed genre type since they both share the same laws and characteristics.

4 Narrative identity and image building in *Z*
A Novel of Zelda Fitzgerald

As noted above, the re-writing of past lives means rediscovering and reinventing the self, the context and the past events. The genre play, in biofictions especially, underlines the idea of interpretation and changeability in telling the life story. Fowler's *Z: A Novel of Zelda Fitzgerald*, as a biofiction of the Fitzgeralds, deals with Fitzgerald's wife Zelda in particular. As such, it is created to take a particular stance or promote a particular aspect of the real-life story by turning it into fiction. The emphasis here is on turning the factual account into an emotional journey of the characters as processed by Zelda's inner sentiments.

The author's interest is, decidedly, to represent Zelda's self-discovery while revisiting the most crucial events in Zelda and Fitzgerald's lives. The recount involves the image of Fitzgerald and Zelda as husband and wife, how they came to be together and how their lives developed. Another specific "bio element" dealt with in this narrative is the exceptional animosity between Zelda and Hemingway. Fowler embarks on the quest to find the explanation for that and presents her own scenario for the story.

These stories are most emphatically told by the first-person narration of the fictional Zelda by developing an intriguing set of a genre play. This aspect coupled with the story's cohesiveness is discernable from the biopreservation sequences. The narrative elements, in turn, are first identified then described and explained.

In both *Z: A Novel of Zelda Fitzgerald* and *Save Me the Waltz*, the authors bring to life the first half of the twentieth century, the modernist era in America and in Paris. They both choose the character of Zelda as the main protagonist. The prologue of *Z: A Novel of Zelda Fitzgerald* begins with the letter Zelda sends to Scott from the sanatorium and his reply. The letters are setting the scene, i.e. the situatedness for the development of the whole story.

The exchange of letters is the first instance of a biopreservation sequence marking the beginning of the story. The epistolary beginning of the narrative amplifies the confessionary aspect by providing a set of thought developments. However, all the letters that appear in the novel are the author's creations, inspired by the amazing body of correspondence in the couple's real lives. That becomes a good example of the postmodern palimpsest or pastiche, prompting the reader to search for the traces of the actual letters exchanged by the couple.

The beginning of *Z: A Novel of Zelda Fitzgerald* underlines the urge of the fictional character to confess her story very much like the real-life Zelda in her *Save Me the Waltz*. The narrative in Fowler's book takes Zelda back to her home in Alabama where she revisits herself as a young woman, almost 18, dancing ballet since the age of nine. Fowler uses this fact to create a fairytale story of a happy Southern family before World War I. This portrayal serves as a foreground for the future developments in her life. The contrast of a carefree family life in the South with the woman she becomes deeply affects Zelda's recount. All she gathers from that period of her life is a happy growing up in the family of her parents, three older sisters and a brother.

This biopreservation sequence can be contrasted with the one presented in *Save Me the Waltz*. In her own book, the real Zelda presents her parents as caring as the ones presented in Fowler's book, but the attention here is put on the parents' serious concern about the future of her two sisters, Joan and Dixie.

When one of her sisters, Joan, is supposed to get married, she has to choose between a rich boy her father approves of and a poorer boy who cannot offer her much but whom she adores. In the end, the sister hesitantly accedes to the proposal by the rich boy, Acton. This situation might reflect Zelda's own dilemma when considering the financial situation of her Fitzgerald prior to their marriage.

In Fowler's book, Zelda's own character and temperament are also shown as visible at a very early age. Her activities, daring for the time, are symbolic of the future break with the tradition and background of the Southern way of life. This is an example of situatedness which enables Zelda to present her own view about herself. In this way, the narrative establishes the first picture of Zelda, i.e. her own image making. She begins by expressing her attitude as a young teenage girl towards going outs, infatuation and boys.

Though the rain was tapering off, the sidewalks were still mostly empty—few witnesses to my dishevelment, then, which would make Mama happy. She worries about the oddest things, I thought. All the women do. There were so many rules we girls were supposed to adhere to, so much emphasis on propriety. Straight backs. Gloved hands. Unpainted (and unkissed) lips. Pressed skirts, modest words, downturned eyes, chaste thoughts. A lot of nonsense, in my view. Boys liked me because I shot spitballs and because I told sassy jokes and because I let 'em kiss me if they smelled nice and I felt like it. My standards were based on good sense, not the logic of lemmings. Sorry, Mama. You're better than most.

(Fowler:3)

On the other hand, in her own novel, Zelda does not give as much independence to Alabama Beggs as her counterpart author does in *Z: A Novel of Zelda Fitzgerald*. Alabama is largely dependent on her older sisters' relations and decisions. She is rather more of a child to them than an adult.

In both books, the central biopreservation sequence in the world making/world disrupting is Zelda's dancing. In Fowler's book, Zelda is portrayed as a restless young girl, full of life and open for new adventures and experiences. Here, this sequence is followed by another one connected to the disruption of the stable world order, the imminent war. She and her girlfriends enroll in the Red Cross activity of packaging medical supplies. The war also brings high circulation of soldiers and officers to their town. Despite the atrocities that wartime has brought, there is nothing more exciting for Zelda and her girlfriends than meeting and dancing with the military men. Zelda is a playful coquette, a well-known southern belle and a serious option for marriage for some of the men she meets.

The image of Alabama, on the other hand, is that of a young girl who gets to flirt around, almost disregarding other people's feelings. These instances of biopreservation sequences built different narrative identities, showing how this specific play can result in various narratives and character building.

Not less important is the building of Fitzgerald's character. One of the first aspects of Fitzgerald's life story presented at the very beginning of *Z: A Novel of Zelda Fitzgerald* is his attitude towards money and the rich.

All my school friends with their millionaire fathers, their houses, their trips abroad, their social class why couldn't I have been born one of them? He looked over at me, and I shroud. I wanted a place at their tables. My writing was supposed to get me there – not the millions, there is no hope of that, but the prestige. In America, you can invent your way to the top of any field. And when you do – well, you're in. He pointed at the letter still in my hand. 'That, my dear girl is the end of a dream.'

(Fowler:82)

Thus, financial anxiety becomes pivotal in Fitzgerald's world making/world disrupting based on the well-known fact that his mother and father had financial difficulties while he was growing up. This becomes also a very good example of how biopreservation sequences serve the purpose of world making/world disrupting in biofiction.

Biopreservation sequences also help mark the situatedness of the narrative as it is in this case. What is more, focusing on that particular fact Zelda finds herself in the position of an (un)willing sacrificial scapegoat for the rest of her life since her own attitude towards money is also determined by that confession as are her later choices.

Confessing his professional troubles becomes also the starting point of Scott's image making in the book. Being financially insecure will make him feel insecure in his relations with people, too. As Donaldson's recounts:

> The lack of physical magnetism troubled Fitzgerald. In the notebooks he assembled during the 1930s, he calculated his personal assets. 'I didn't have the two top things – great animal magnetism or money. I had the two second things, tho', good looks and intelligence. So, I always got the top girl.
>
> (Donaldson 1999:32)

In this way, both Zelda's and Fitzgerald's images become interdependent and turn into an integral part of Zelda's narrative identity which is built on the basis of biopreservation sequences. They help construct the specific world making/world disruption, the event sequencing and what it is like elements in Fowler's novel. They involve the couple, their family, friends, the people and places they visit as well as the time when they lived. Fowler uses this specific genre play of fact and fiction not just to refer to her characters, but to place them in a particular context. In this sense, she turns the couple's romantic story into an essential aspect of their lives. Their meeting, for example, set in the Montgomery Country Club, is a scene in what would become an epic story. Fitzgerald's deployment there is the biopreservation basis for illustrating Zelda's infatuation and falling in love with him.

> While taking my bows, I noticed the officers at the front of the crowd. Like others I'd met, these fellas were little older than my usual beaux. Their uniforms, with those serious brass buttons and knee-high leather boots, gave them sophistication that the local boys – even the ones in college – were lacking.... A pair of tall boots paler than the others caught my eye. As I straightened, I followed the boots upward to olive-colored breeches, a fitted uniform tunic, and, above it, an angelic face with eyes as green and expressive as the Irish Sea, eyes that snagged and held me surely as a bug sticks in a web, eyes that contain the entire world in their smiling depths.
>
> (Fowler:21)

This revelation renders Zelda as an emotional but strong woman, one who has worked over her youthful fallacies. It shows how she moves from *contamination* to *agency*. This particular pattern turns into a dominant theme around which her narrative revolves. In between, there are the necessary episodes of the *exploratory narrative processing* and a resulting *positive resolution* and *meaning making* whenever possible.

The narrative continues in the emotional vein, the whole scene of their fatal infatuation presented in the most romantic way.

> He danced as well as any of my partners ever had – better, maybe. It seemed to me that the energy I was feeling that night had infused him, too; we glided through the waltz as if we'd been dancing together for years.
>
> (Fowler:24)

This sequence strongly underlines Zelda's narrative identity. In support of different image projections, Fowler uses parodic irony through parodic intertextuality in this passage.

The next important biopreservation sequence is connected with Fitzgerald's strive for fame and glamour both for himself and for the one he loves. This is part of the event sequencing that marks the celebration of Zelda's 18th birthday. Fitzgerald himself organizes the party that would turn out to be big and expensive, something that he could have hardly afforded at that time but is part of his insecurity and attempt to win the heart of his beloved. It adds a significant nuance to Fitzgerald's character building in the novel and underscores Zelda's attempt to make a choice. While trying to evaluate her options, the fictional Zelda muses over her life in the South without Scott, trying to take into consideration her family's and especially her mother's opinion. She is presented as a romantic figure that is about to embark on a journey. This breaking point is filled with romantic sadness and suspense. Her getting the flu in this particular period is symbolic of the difficulty of the situation and what might ensue. Based on "bio" facts as we know them from Donaldson's and Fitzgerald's accounts, the biopreservation sequence used by Fowler constructs a narrative identity which differs from the existing accounts as the next paragraph shows.

> Zelda delayed committing herself to Scott until he could demonstrate sufficient capacity to support her. When she broke off their engagement on those grounds, he wrote in a *Crack-Up* essay of 1936, it seemed to be "one of those tragic loves doomed for lack of money." In the end he won Zelda back by publishing a novel and selling a story to Hollywood. But, he pointed out, "since then I have never been able to stop wondering where my friends› money came from, nor to stop thinking that at some time a sort of *droit de seigneur* might have been exercised to give one of them my girl." The images of both Zelda and Ginevra must have conflated in his mind as he wrote those words, though the courtships hardly resembled each other. Zelda came from an old Southern family, but she was by no means rich. And she always took Scott seriously as a suitor, even when she was putting him off. Ginevra, apparently, never did.
>
> (Donaldson 1999:36)

Despite the fact that financial concerns are at the center of the biopreservation sequence that would seem to be a breaking point in Fitzgerald's life, it is Zelda's narrative identity that is built differently in Fowler's text and she emerges as the stronger and more responsible figure. "He sat down on the top step – drooped onto it, as if the rejection had softened his bones, "You know, I was the worst student as a kid. No concentration. [...] my father has a name but not real money " (Fowler:37). It is clear that Fitzgerald's personal narrative coding constructs are most often either *contamination* or *agency* as this example shows.

The fact that Scott gets a contract for publishing gives him the boost to go on and seek a brighter future for him and his bride-to-be. This "bio" element is taken to present them in the novel as unstoppable. To begin with, the moment when Zelda arrives in New York with her sister to arrange the marital ceremony, is presented as magic. Zelda's initial fascination with everything around her can be compared with that of Alice in Wonderland. She is impressed by every place she sees and every person she meets which allows Fowler to render Zelda's narrative identity in progression. At this point, she is portrayed as a childish girl that is given to Scott to be educated and transformed, to grow up. The story turns into one of a modern American couple living to the fullest. Their great love, social gatherings and making the best of every moment is strongly emphasized in the narrative, only to be contrasted with minor disturbances and their personal and professional problems.

On the other hand, Zelda's arrival in New York in *Save Me the Waltz* is less dramatic. Alabama travels alone to New York to meet David Knight, the famous painter. Nevertheless, for the time, the author leaves us with the high-society adventures of the newly-weds. In both narratives, their hearts pulsate in the same rhythm. The blissful times of their marriage are presented to explain how and why the Fitzgeralds are going to become an era. The account of the fictional Zelda is more emphatic and emotional, only to be contrasted with the inevitable dissolution.

In both books, the couple seems to be in accordance with everything around them, especially the taste of the roaring twenties. Social gatherings are the day's news. In Fowler's book, Zelda's intertextual and parodic irony accounts for her opinion on meeting all the new people.

> This group, and this bookish world in which they lived and were simultaneously creating, was a collegiate literary circle puffed into wide proportions by the New York magazines and papers; that's how I saw it before long...With this group, though, and their counterparts from Yale, and the postwar push for life, for fun, for all the things Scott and I were seeking and embodying, the literary world put its foot into the circle of the entertainment world's spotlight. Not far; far enough, though, for the public to see the polished, well-cut shoe and wonder to whom it might belong.
>
> (Fowler:96)

Yet, she romanticizes the part that suggests that all there was in that world was purely romantic. Zelda's concluding opinion in this section wraps up her endless raving with her husband.

> Just then, though, that influential little group was still a bunch of young, ambitious, intelligent men, along with me, a very young woman who hadn't known there would be this kind of carnival and wasn't sure she even wanted to ride the Ferris wheel – but was game enough to give it a try.
>
> (Fowler:97)

To emphasize the difference between Zelda's new life with Fitzgerald and her old Southern life, Fowler introduces a scene of Zelda meeting up an old friend in New York.

> 'Gene!' I said, not simply glad to see an old friend, but glad to see someone from home – except the thought of home, of my mama and all my friends, suddenly made me wish I hadn't seen Gene after all.
>
> (Fowler:104)

Here, Zelda breaks with her old life, entering the unknown future. Zelda makes a *positive coherent resolution*, although only implicitly noted.

Another biopreservation sequence marks the point of culmination of the couple's drinking and partying around. More specifically, there is the moment Zelda entering the fountain near Union Square to show how daring and courageous she was. The scene is presented as the result of a mixture of "green substance". Donaldson also accounts for this moment:

> Fitzgerald's characters drank and smoked, open and recklessly opposed of the older generation. So did Scott and Zelda Fitzgerald themselves, as if determined to become public avatars of the flappers and sheiks in his fashion. Living in, or around New York, they dwindled into celebrities as the newspapers eagerly recorded their nocturnal exploits – most notably a midnight dip in the fountain outside the Plaza Hotel. They came to Europe in the spring of 1924 in order to escape the frantic partying, but geography could not alter Fitzgerald's public image. For the rest of his life – and beyond – he fought vainly

to shake off his reputation as a rather lightweight chronicler of the Jazz Age.

(Donaldson 1999:53)

In Fowler's book (p. 104), this "bio" element marks their first days of marriage. The mixture of "green substance" is suggestive both of alcohol and jealousy, but only in Fowler's book, it is Zelda who is jealous of other women paying attention to Scott. She does not hesitate to remind him that he is what he is because of her. This is another example of Zelda's sacrificial position in relation to her husband.

The Fitzgeralds never got to settle in only one place. In one of the houses where they lived, they had a Japanese boy as a servant. This fact is preserved in both *Z: A Novel of Zelda Fitzgerald* and *Save Me the Waltz*. In both books, the authors introduce the scene of Zelda's parents visiting them. There is a certain debauchery scene with drunken guests visiting them with two distinct endings in both narratives. Both Zelda and Alabama end up with a black eye. Zelda in *Zelda: A Novel of Zelda Fitzgerald* considers it to be a normal fight, one like her childish fights with her siblings, while in *Save Me the Waltz*, Alabama accidentally hurts herself and ends up wounded. In both cases, she is not specifically worried about her parents seeing her in that condition, nor is she concerned about them assuming the worst of their marriage. Their drunken times seem never-ending and that situation is one of the consequences. Contrary to the other passages, in this episode, Zelda's attitude as the victim is not visible at all. Here she makes a coherent positive resolution of her role in the incident while showing a surprising resilience.

In both narratives, Zelda and Alabama go on to assume their role as they deem most fitting for their position. They see themselves as celebrities, the way the New York society comes to accept them. Fowler intertextually uses Scott's short story "Bernice Bobs Her Hair" to show how ready Zelda is for new adventures when she gets her new bob hairstyle. The events gain intensity with numerous meetings, talks and introduction. There are scenes of partying, descriptions of people coming with a possibility for Zelda to become an actress.

As a result of the couple's restlessness, they decide to go to Paris. This moment is another example of a biopreservation sequence. In Fowler's book, they meet Winston Churchill and his mother on board a ship to Europe, while in Donaldson's account they only meet Churchill's mother. There is no mentioning of either one of these people in *Save Me the Waltz*, nor anything about their first trip to Europe.

This event in Fowler's narrative is sequenced by their return to America. They go back to Scott's family house where they are placed in another setting, a possible idyllic family life with their baby daughter. Part of this narrative is the sequence when Zelda gets pregnant for the second time but decides to end it. While she is at Scott's home, she is eager to write. She deems herself serious and productive while staying there.

Zelda's narration shifts from money problems to reference to Scott's story "How to Live on $36,000 a Year". Going to Paris where they could live a luxurious life for little money becomes their best option and they decide to take the advantage of it. A decisive moment at this point is the introduction of Esther Murphy, who mentions her brother and sister-in-law, Gerald and Sara Murphy to the Fitzgeralds, suggesting they meet them when they go in Paris. The Murphys become an emblematic example of marital bliss for the Fitzgeralds and the Hemingways alike. Fowler uses their ideal rich life in France to point out the differences and possible flaws of the marital life of Zelda and Fitzgerald. This part also serves to emphasize Zelda's social side and how she values others. Her identity here is marked by this *communion*.

The next event sequence takes Fowler's narrative to Europe. Shortly after their arrival in France, the Fitzgeralds are set to become the official American expatriates. Settling in Saint Raphael on the French Riviera, Scott feels this would be the place that would make him great. It was also the first time Zelda feels that she lost track of herself.

> The first time I lost track of myself, truly lost all trace of me, the girl I'd been, the woman I thought I was becoming, would happen there in Saint Raphael, while I was wrapped in the benevolent warmth of a Mediterranean summer. The romantic ending to our night on the terrace was a romantic ending, period.
> (Fowler:170)

This is the introduction of the scene that also takes place in both *Tender Is the Night* and *Save Me the Waltz*. However, *Save Me the Waltz* was published two years earlier than Scott's novel *Tender Is the Night* (1934). This part represents a breaking point in Zelda's narrative. Zelda's delicate condition is the most debatable issue that irreparably affects the couple's lives. Her rather covert revelation of her problem at this point is the beginning of her redemption and recovery.

This scene is followed by the event of Zelda becoming infatuated with a young aviator. This is also part of Zelda's own book as well as Scott's novel. In Fowler's book, the foreign country certainly brings something foreign for Zelda. She becomes attracted to a young French aviator, Edouard Jozan:

> The aviators we knew from the casino also began to come to the beach, three, Eduard, Rene and Bobbe. Their schedules had them training at night. They would arrive in their white, white beach clothes and put their mats down near mine, and we'd talk, them with their iffy English, me with my slowly improving French.
>
> (Fowler:172)

The connection that develops between Zelda and Jozan becomes serious and they start a relationship. Zelda's growing detachment from Scott and enchantment with the French aviator leads to her asking for a divorce. Scott is shocked and surprised:

> I want a husband who cares about me more than anything else, except his children maybe. With you, it's always the next story, play, novel, movie, the unending pursuit of some stupid critic's approval, an obsession over some magical number of copies sold, a terrible need for assurance that you're the finest living writer on the planet and every thinking man will worship your books forever!
>
> (Fowler:180)

Through intertextual parody, this episode further builds Scott's image as a struggling writer and husband. While he is asking Zelda for another chance, she is thinking of her chance with Jozan. Fowler settles this dispute with Zelda's decision to stay. "I wasn't in love with him, not really. Edouard was a symbol; Edouard was a symptom. Scott, for all his shortcomings, owned my heart" (Fowler:186). These lines echo Zelda's *narrative processing* and the resulting *positive resolution* to this life-changing dilemma.

The matter is settled peacefully with Zelda figuring out her obsession. She stops going to the beach or sending notes to Jozan. Upon finding out that Jozan was heartbroken and confused and would not forget her, she says, "now he is a member of a very prestigious club" (Fowler:188).

In *Save Me Waltz*, Lieutenant Jacques Chevre-Feuille of the French Aviation was the man who absorbed Alabama's attention during a night of dancing. The confrontation between David and the lieutenant gets almost physical. The matter ends when Jacques decides to leave for Indochina.

Another biopreservation sequence is Scott's publication of *The Great Gatsby*, the novel that would establish him as one of the most important American novelists. However, *The Great Gatsby* is not given much attention in Fowler's novel, Zelda is only mentioned as the one who gives the title to the book. Instead, the attention is put on their leaving for Paris again, by contrasting their marital bliss with the destruction caused by Hemingway. The choices of the biofiction author reflect the tendency of the postmodernist narrative to inflate and deflate certain episodes and characters, by giving them different narrative treatments. Here, Zelda's *coherent resolution* directly involves an undisputable culprit, Hemingway. Both of these events are missing in *Save Me the Waltz*.

To that end, in the biopreservation sequence involving the couple's meeting with Hemingway, Fowler adds events and characters leaving space for new interpretations by filling the gaps in the story.

> I rested my head against his shoulder and we watched the sunset, just like you might see in the movies. We'd worked hard to create this lovely, new domestic bliss, and before Gatsby's publication, right up until the book was printed and put into the hands of both the reading and the reviewing public, it looked as if we might actually succeed. Wait: if I leave it at that, it'll sound like the novel's disappointing performance is to blame for the disaster we made of our lives, and that's not so Ernest Hemingway is to blame.
>
> (Fowler:190)

The event of Hemingway–Fitzgerald meeting is such a sequence of discursive pluralizing, since it is a major event in the lives of the two authors.

> We got acquainted with Hemingway the writer before we met Hemingway the man. Bob McAlmon, a scrappy writer and publisher we'd first met when we were in London and saw again

in Capri, had done a small printing of Hemingway's work the year before and mentioned him to Scott. McAlmon said Hemingway was a true talent, 'though he's having a damnably hard time getting the attention of the *Post*.'

(Fowler:200)

During that time, Scott tracks down some copies of Hemingway's work and decides to put him forward to his publisher Maxwell Perkins. A new age of Scott's life will start on that mission. At the same time, Zelda's narrative starts to shape Fitzgerald's character more substantially.

In Fowler's narrative, at the first meeting with Hemingway, when Pound introduces them at the Dingo, Zelda has an initial negative feeling towards him. Fowler contrasts that with her positive attitude towards Pound, although she condemns his polygamy on several occasions.

Fowler further builds Fitzgerald's image on the back of Hemingway's presence in their lives. As Scott and Hemmingway begin their friendship, Scott becomes absorbed in continuing and developing the matter of consultations, writing and publishing and Zelda also becomes agitated. She tells Scott, "That Hemingway, just oozes manliness, doesn't he? All that talk about fishing and hunting and skinning that you catch" (Fowler:215). Scott's reply to this is that of a friend justifying Hemingway's character: "He's an outdoorsman; that's what outdoorsmen do" (Fowler:215).

Fowler uses intertextual parody to undermine Hemingway's image as a macho man. When Zelda compares Hemingway with the boys who did all those things that Hemingway claims to have done and not brag about it, she goes to say: "I mean, really, he's a writer who lives in Paris, that's what he is, just like the rest of them, just like you" (Fowler:215).

The picture of Hemingway becomes more complete when the Fitzgeralds meet the other half of the Hemingways, his first wife, Hadley Richardson.

> When she'd opened the apartment door, her appearance had shocked me nearly as much as the building's horrible, stinking stairway had. I'd imagined someone pert and sweet like Sara Mayfield back home, or else one of those simmering, sultry types, like Tallu. Hadley was neither of those, nor any other type you might think would win herself a handsome, energetic he-man.

(Fowler:218)

In *The Paris Wife*, this episode is presented quite differently, with reverse roles of the two couples.

Another biopreservation sequence in Fowler's narrative is the visit to Gertrude Stein's salon; the whole atmosphere is depicted as one of a modern artists' den. More importantly, that particular atmosphere is used to depict Hadley and Zelda's place in the ex-patriate artistic life in Paris. Hadley is presented as a woman who recognizes that she is just the wife and does not have anything much to do with art: "I'm not a writer, or an artist either. I wouldn't have much to contribute" (Fowler:220). In contrast, Zelda says: "I was both – which neither Scott nor I seemed capable of pointing out, here in the revered Miss Stein's apartment" (Fowler:221).

The event of having Hemingway in their lives, is ironically presented as a bad influence on Scott. Scott's writerly tantrums start to become more common and exacerbate after he befriends Hemingway. At the same time, his jealousy of his wife also starts to bother the couple. Fowler introduces Scott's drinking to make the humiliation even greater. He is jealous of Zelda's friendship with Larionov. Such setting leads to the event of one of the couple's fights. The Murphys, who serve as checks and balances for them, witness this quarrel. After being reprimanded by Gerald Murphy, Scott yells that he is the husband, poking his own chest and stumbling backward a step. In this way, Fitzgerald assumes the image of a drunk and unstable husband who is no longer only his wife's problem, but also a nuisance for their circle of friends. This biopreservation sequence marks much of Fitzgerald's conduct, with his humiliation, his self-ridiculing and apologizing afterwards. As a result a powerful depiction of Fitzgerald's character, of the kind of person he was, influences the way Zelda sees her situation, i.e. she becomes disillusioned which marks resulting *contamination*.

In addition to acting like his agent, Fitzgerald often lends Hemingway money. Fowler uses the moment of Hemingway's bragging about how important he is for Fitzgerald, in order to introduce the crucial scene of Hemingway making a move on Zelda. It is the sequence that marks the specific relations in the Zelda–Fitzgerald–Hemingway triangle.

> Hemingway put his free hand on my shoulder, then slid it down my arm to my wrist, which he gripped tightly. 'All the men want you, you know.' [...] 'I am a man.' He maneuvered us so that my back was pressed against a door and he pressed against me. His interest in me, or at least in sex, was plain. He put his palms on

the wall, bracketing me between his arms. 'It's man's nature to prove himself, to take what he desires.'

(Fowler:232–233)

Zelda rejects him by humiliating his manhood. This significant point subverts and dismantles the myth about the relations between the two couples and reasserts the figures of both Zelda and Hemingway. Hemingway is portrayed as disrespectful towards the Fitzgeralds, while Zelda is the assertive and sober character in the conflict. "I underestimated how astute Hemingway was, how much he already knew about us: He had seen into Scott's soft heart and knew what hapless prey he'd be if he should decide to attack" (Fowler:233). This is another crucial element in Zelda's narrative. It is a powerful *exploratory narrative processing* and a powerful scene that renders Zelda as the responsible agent.

Fowler gives Zelda a chance to change the focus of her story and offers a break for a moment, by placing her in Spain on a recovery from colitis. Upon returning to Paris, Zelda hears a gossip about herself, about her going crazy, and the name of Hemingway is involved, which is when she learns that he could have started the gossip and suspects Pauline of spreading it. Scott, though, does not believe that Hemingway was spreading the story, again underlining their differing positions towards Hemingway.

Zelda assumes that all of their friends seem to know about her marital situation and the Murphys give their support. The Murphys also take care of Hadley and her son while Hemingway is in America figuring out the final break-up. In Fowler's book, however, everybody seems to be more on Hadley's side, although the Murphys seem to be impartial.

Another biopreservation sequence building Zelda's narrative identity is her observation of the polygamy and betrayals of other great artistic figures from their surroundings:

> Maybe I was alone in finding all these things distasteful. Maybe Hadley would be as acquiescent as Stella was, and Dorothy Pound. Maybe she'd be fine with sharing her extra-manly man. I sure couldn't predict the outcome; any woman who was willing to take Hemingway in the first place was a mystery to me.
>
> (Fowler:245)

It is a known fact that Pound had a long-lasting affair with Olga Rudge, while married with Dorothy Shakespear.

Nevertheless, Zelda is also portrayed as a daring and an ex-centric member of the group. She is no stranger to making extraordinary gestures such as climbing on a chair and taking off her panties at a party for Mr. Woollcott's farewell. She does that as her gift to him. This is another example of Zelda's *coherent positive resolution* after grasping the consequences of her behavior.

> Hold on everybody. Here you all are talking about Mr. Woollcott with praise that I'm sure he appreciates, but it seems kind of like you're shortchanging him, don't you think? Where I come from, which is very highly traditional place in America called the state of Alabama, we never send our friends off without also giving them a gift.
>
> (Fowler:249)

The problems the couple have with money is another instance for world making/world disrupting. The troubles start to occur as Scott is struggling with short stories and not starting another novel. Hemingway is placed amid those troubles. This situation is another one in the pile that characterize Hemingway and Fitzgerald, the former making use of the good nature of the other.

> At the casino, Hemingway looked different than he had when I'd seen him last. Smug in one way, and watchful in another. Thanks in large part to Scott, he'd taken a great stride forward in his career and likely had a sense that things were going to improve even more in times to come – but he'd also begun shedding some of the very people whose friendship, guidance and influence had led to his progress [...] While I sought distraction, Scott couldn't seem to separate himself from the attention his great good friend was commanding. Every time I glanced across the room, there he was at Hemingway's elbow [...] If Hemingway was the king that night, then Scott was the court jester – or he tried to be, at least.
>
> (Fowler:253)

The above is Fowler's attempt to underline and offer a final judgment of the nature of the two authors. In addition, Gerald Murphy throws Scott out when Scott's making a fool of himself reaches a breaking point. Again, this is underlined by an intertextual parody of the Scott–Hemingway friendship.

> When I saw Scott next, he was attempting to juggle three glass ashtrays and was managing pretty well until some man I didn't recognize called out, 'Say, Fitzgerald, when are you ever going to write another book?' Scott threw one of the ashtrays at the offender, grazing the man's head, 'Enough!' Gerald hissed. He took Scott's arm and led him toward the door. 'You might have killed him. Christ almighty, Scott, go home and sleep it off.' [...]Scott's eyes brimmed with tears. 'I'm sorry.' Gerald turned from him and Scott clutched his hand. 'I'm sorry. Please, don't make me leave.'
>
> (Fowler:254)

Another instance of preserving Hemingway's image as an unfaithful macho and Hadley as a humble wife suffering from her husband's infidelity is the conversation between Zelda and Hadley: "'Oh Zelda,' she said when she saw me, 'I'm the biggest fool. Ernest and Pauline have been carrying on for God knows how long, he doesn't even deny it. What am I supposed to do with this?'" (Fowler:254).

The struggle for money leads to preserving the episode when they go to Hollywood to sell some of Scott's works. Their brief two-month stay there is marked by Scott's interest in a young actress. It presents some of the material for *Tender Is the Night* and as such is interwoven into Zelda's story as another of her disillusions. To further intensify her bad condition, back in Paris, Zelda decides to assume ballet lessons despite her older age.

Further illustration of Zelda harboring many suspicions regarding the friendship between her husband and Hemingway results from her hearing Fitzgerald say Hemingway's name in a dream. She decides to go through his letters and materials to find some clue on their relations. She fails to find any, noting only variations of Hemingway's style. She too feels that Hemingway resents Fitzgerald's role as his mentor.

> Even with my resentment, knowing that Scott was struggling with his novel troubled me. It was a dilemma: his drinking habits prevented him from working on anything that required more than a day or two's attention, while his inability to do more than produce more short stories demeaned him in his own eyes – which made him want to drink more. Getting tight soothed

the insecurities that Hemingway had cued into so quickly and so well; but they came raging back if he indulged too much. I felt bad for Scott in one way, impatient with him in a whole bunch of others. Where was the man I'd married?

(Fowler:295)

The scene with the stopwatch is another such portrait of the two friends also preserved in Fowler's narrative. Scott is supposed to keep watch of the time in Hemingway and Morley's fight. Hemingway loses, but Scott forgets to call time. Hemingway is furious, while Fitzgerald is afraid that he disappointed his "friend".

Another image pairing is created when Fowler introduces the story about Zelda's dance lessons and the invitation to work in Naples as another reason for the dispute between the spouses. Fitzgerald does not let Zelda take the job. When Zelda says that she would go anyway and take their daughter with her, Scott rejects the possibility, threatening to keep Scottie with himself. After due consideration and thought of legal rights, Zelda refuses the offer to go to Naples.

In contrast to this, in *Save Me the Waltz* Alabama does go to Naples to perform for the opera. She becomes successful, but she is away from her family. When her daughter comes to visit, although she is having a great time, she feels better with the rich life beside her father. In the end, Alabama suffers an accident with her toe leading to infection which prevents her from further performing.

This sequence is yet another example of Zelda's sacrificial role in her marriage. Nonetheless, narrating it renders her a winner who had overcome the problem and not an inconsolable and regretful victim.

Zelda's health condition is yet another biopreservation sequence used for world making/world disrupting and event sequencing. On a night out with the Murphys, Zelda feels serious restlessness and agitation. She cannot see clearly around her nor the screen of the movie theater. The condition turns out to be serious. It is established as schizophrenia as she is taken in a Swiss hospital in Geneva. This is a moment embodied in *Tender Is the Night*. Zelda starts to write in Geneva and the recollections are presented in the book. Hoping that leaving Europe would alleviate the situation, Zelda goes to America where she visits other clinics. At the John Hopkins hospital, she decides to write a book. The writing of her own book, *Save Me the Waltz* attests to that fact.

Fictional Zelda's narrative goes on with her being forbidden by the doctors to write. She turns to painting instead. Scott organizes a great exhibition of her work. Her novel *Save Me Waltz* is also published, but none of these things seems overtly successful and she feels like a failure. Scott is struggling to provide enough money in Hollywood for his wife's treatments, struggling to write his novel while also struggling with alcohol. He is as miserable as Zelda at times.

Being in and out of clinics Zelda decides to grasp what would appear as their last stand, feeling better at the not-so-high-profile Highland clinic. There she seems to manage to understand who she is. Fowler builds suspense before the final acts: "For the first time in a decade both Scott and I are free. And now I wait" (Fowler:360).

Zelda's narrative identity further takes the turn to an utter failure, a state of disillusionment and disappointment. Therefore, presenting a ruined atmosphere of their glamorous years in Europe, of death in her family and the families of their dear friends, Fowler takes Zelda back to her parents' house in Alabama. The consolation and warmth of her family is used as a metaphor for Zelda's life journey:

> In the deep, wet, tangled, wild jungle where even natives won't go is a mystical dangerous river. The river's got no name because naming it would make it real, and no one wants to believe that river be real. They say you get there only inside a dream – but you think of it at bedtime, now, cause not everyone who go there be able to leave! Scot was in the river too.
>
> (Fowler:362)

Just before finding out about Scott's death, Zelda walks around the streets where she grew up. This is probably the most personal contemplation of their life together.

> There is the corner where Scott proposed to me. Suppose I'd gone home that night and decided that, no, I stood to lose more than I might gain by taking such risk? In that alternate world, there might be no Paradise, no Gatsby, none of the hundreds or more published stories that readers so love. Ernest Hemingway might yet be poor and little known. And my life, it would look like Marjorie's: safe and predictable and unexceptional and dull. Even now, I wouldn't choose differently than I did.
>
> (Fowler:363)

This is the authors' alternative to end the turbulent story between the remarkable couple. The final biopreservation sequence is one that underlines the fact and fiction play in all of the previous episodes and narrative elements. It concludes Zelda's own journey through life and her final *positive coherent resolution*. The whole narrative identity is built on a roller coaster of events and conditions all properly marked by the narrative sequences. In this way, Fowler masterfully builds the fictional narrative identity of one of the most emblematic women in the twentieth century. Her life story is all the more challenging as it intersects many other people's life choices, trips, successes, failures, illnesses and deaths. In particular, her diagnosis with schizophrenia leaves this narrative unique in the attempt to create a compelling personal story. Fictional Zelda's account of her life story replicates carefully selected aspects of Zelda's life easing along the biopreservation sequences to form a new image of real-life Zelda.

The above analysis enables us to see the different narrative identity elements sieved through the narratives of both the real and the fictional Zelda. They all seem to meet into one unity in order to uncover the inner selves of the narrators. We can see how certain moments in Scott and Zelda's lives are exalted into emotions of significance, of breaking points and necessary positive resolutions. As a result, the reader is compelled to acknowledge unique revelations, images and narrative identities. All this confirms the importance of the genre play in life-writing as it structurally uncovers its textuality in the form of biopreservation. This is further confirmed in the following analytical account on the biofictions under study.

5 Narrative identity and image building in *The Paris Wife*

Paula McLain's *The Paris Wife* touches upon a very specific time of Hemingway's life when he was at his best: young, happy and in Paris. Throughout his life, his attitude towards that period would remain the same, and he would always remember this period with affection:

> There is never any ending to Paris and the memory of each person who has lived in it differs from that of any other. We always returned to it no matter who we were or how it was changed or with what difficulties, or ease, it could be reached. Paris was always worth it and you received return for whatever you brought to it. But this is how Paris was in the early days when we were very poor and very happy.
> (Hemingway 1964:236)

Moreover, he was newly married and was enjoying Paris with Hadley Richardson, who is the protagonist in *The Paris Wife*. His biographers would not always describe her as the perfect wife for him, since she seemingly did not care much for his work, maybe because he was still at the beginning of his writing career and his talent was just starting to flourish. She would lose his four-year work on her way to visiting him in Switzerland where he was on an assignment. However, she did not do that intentionally but rather carelessly, and although years of Hemingway's effort and creativity were invested in those scripts, he was not mad at his wife:

> I had never seen anyone hurt by a thing other than death or unbearable suffering except Hadley when she told me about the things being gone. She had cried and cried and could not tell me. I told her that no matter what the dreadful thing was that

had happened nothing could be that bad, and whatever it was, it was all right and not to worry. We could work it out. Then, finally, she told me [...] It was probably good for me to lose early work [...] I was going to start writing stories again...

(Hemingway 1964:69)

This specific moment attests to the strengthening of their loving relationship. Nevertheless, marriage for both of them meant not only the growth of their affection but also growing apart. It is, however, certain that without their time together, nothing would have been the same for either of them. In her later interviews, Hadley claimed that she exploded into life when she came across Hemingway. She was grateful for the world that was opened up for her but also recognized that the divorce was a great relief for her (Diliberto 2011). They formed a comfortable couple in contrast with the Fitzgeralds. As discussed in the previous chapter, Zelda clearly put forward her ambition and dwindled in the ever-growing competitiveness with her husband.

All of these facts and the whole aura around Hemingway's persona are the basis of *The Paris Wife*. The narrator in this book is interestingly not Hemingway but Hadley. She is the wife that brings him back to "normal" life after the war and stays with him until he writes his first great novel, *The Sun Also Rises*. She is the wife who befriends the Fitzgeralds and some of the other people around Hemingway, who gives birth to their first child and travels across the Atlantic with him.

Although the narrative is in first person, like the one in *Z: A Novel of Zelda Fitzgerald*, the tone of the narration is different. The author presents Hadley as a mature woman who despite the unhappy ending of their marital life renders herself as a winner. That is the underlying narrative identity McLain builds of Hadley Richardson in her biofiction.

Unlike Zelda, who has trouble accepting the marriage proposal from Fitzgerald, Hadley readily takes Hemingway's proposal. She sees herself as the more mature one in the couple. This initial notion is present throughout the whole story and serves the purpose of dismantling the myth of Hemingway as a person who is at the center of attention and has everything under control. To present young Hemingway's and Hadley's views about single life and marriage, McLain intertextually weaves events from the characters' past as well as material from Hemingway's own novels in numerous biopreservation sequences thus constructing a tale of their lives that builds up different narrative identities from what earlier biographers have done.

A characteristic feature of the events that McLain has chosen to use as biopreservation sequences is that no matter whether they happened or appear to have happened they are intrinsically connected to her commitment to give her readers a novel perspective on the Hemingways. One of the ways in which she does that is to use intertextuality to deconstruct Hemingway's heroic figure and show Hadley as the stronger in this relation subverting the past. The novel is full of numerous such compositional devices to establish the biopreservation sequences by integrating the purely factual and the purely fictional. One of these instances is Hemingway's past as a war veteran. As the two are getting to know each other, Hemingway mentions the war and his part in it to Hadley. In a very open account of his war experience and his love affair in Italy in his first conversations with Hadley, it becomes clear that his broken heart, more than the pain caused by the wounds, is the reason for most of his choices. This sequence forms the *world making/world disrupting* of the narrative. As such, it formulates Hadley's attitude towards Hemingway and makes her accept him as her life partner. This is the beginning of Hadley's subtle growth from a sacrificial wife to a reliable agent who confidently makes *positive coherent resolutions* about her life with Hemingway.

Another example of the use of intertextuality as a way of building up of biopreservation sequences is Hemingway's boxing ambitions from an early age. Following the known facts, amid Hemingway and Hadley's courtship, McLain inserts a scene of boxing as a spontaneous match between friends which, although good-naturedly, accentuates Hemingway's desire to win.

To further the process of building Hemingway's character, McLain introduces not only Hadley's perspective but also her friend's opinion of Hemingway which seems to reveal a tendency of Hemingway to seduce different women. McLain installs a moment suggesting Hemingway's seductive nature by inserting his flirting with Hadley's friend Kate. This is supposed to warn Hadley. It also serves a double purpose: to add to Hemingway's character building and to show Hadley's self-confidence despite being warned by her friend about Hemingway's character (see McLain:46).

This whole episode, however, becomes suggestive of his future behavior with women and gives Hadley's perspective on a marriage that was going to end in divorce. However, before that happens Hadley would continue to be fascinated by Hemingway who tries to project an image of a writer who desires to offer something unlike anything before him and believes that he has created his own writing style. This is quite evident in the episode in which he asks Hadley to read his stuff and give her opinion, aptly mentioning Henry James to make a point (see McLain:37).

The fact that the fictional Hadley makes a connection between Hemingway and Henry James is another example of intertextuality and how it works in creating biopreservation sequences. As Neal B. Houston writes in 1985,

> he [Hemingway] was often to refer to James in highly derisive terms – almost to the end of his own life. Hemingway's *lèse majesté* towards him [Henry James] takes the form of a sporadic obsession that reveals more about Hemingway's maturity than James' imagined frailties.
>
> (Houston 1985:33)

Moreover, as Carlos Baker vividly describes it, "Ernest Hemingway squirmed as his second wife, Pauline, read aloud in 1927 from Henry James's novel *The Awkward Age*" (Baker 1968:243). All this play becomes a telling example of how the factual floats into the fictional and still preserves its authenticity.

If we dig further, we can discover more of this ambiguous attitude of Hemingway towards Henry James and how it has been used in postmodern fiction. If we look at the way the main character in *A Farewell to Arms* speaks about the war, it is striking that he uses the same words that Henry James used in his first and only interview in the *New York Times* from 1915. As Susan Griffin has observed:

> The war disturbs James's relation with language. He complains that he cannot bring himself to write fiction. Attempting to describe the American Volunteer Motor Ambulance Corps' tasks in an interview, he laments 'The war has used up words […] they have, like millions of other things, been more overstrained and knocked about and voided of the happy semblance during the last six months than in all the long ages before, and we are now confronted with the deprecation of all our terms.'
>
> (167)

Ernest Hemingway copied part of this interview, giving his main character the line, "Abstract words such as glory, honor, courage, or hallow were obscene beside the concrete names of villages, the number of roads, the names of rivers, the numbers of regiments and dates" (Hemingway 1929: 184–185). McLain seems to have done the same in her novel, creating what postmodern critics such as Jean Baudrillard have called the *simulacrum,* the existence of a copy without an original, "the simulacrum is never that which conceals the truth—it is the truth which conceals that there is none. The simulacrum is true" (Baudrillard 1988:166).

This is even more obvious in the barely noticeable slip from fact to fiction that is one of the most characteristic features of biofiction, as represented by the fictitious letters Hemingway writes to Hadley talking about his parents. Choosing the epistolary mode and creating a postmodern pastiche, Paula McLain offers convincing and undivided moments of sharing between the two, which adds to the close and intimate relationship developing between the future spouses. There are, in fact, letters that have survived from the early 1920s that Hemingway sent to his father and wife from Lausanne (Hemingway 2003:74–76), that have become the basis of the letters McLain creates. In them, Hemingway talks about his father and mother who are presented with different affection. He admires and adores his father and the time they spent hunting and fishing, while his mother is presented as dominant, criticizing and in a way controlling person (see McLain:76). Although fictitious, for the reader, these letters allow a glimpse into the very private sphere of such relations and Hadley's most open revelations.

Another biopreservation sequence starting with the factual and moving into the imaginary is the moment when Hemingway is offered an opportunity to go to Rome with a friend and this becomes a decisive point in his life. He turns down this job opportunity because it would separate him from Hadley. In the book, this is romanticized in order to emphasize the connection between the two. "'If your work is the thing that matters most, you should go.' I tried to meet his eyes squarely over the table. 'But a girl would miss you.' He nodded seriously but didn't say anything" (McLain:83).

Simultaneously, by use of intertextuality, historical and literary texts are restored, sometimes historical ones within literary texts and vice versa, locating them in another ever-expanding intertextual network. The notions of reference and their textual causality are questioned. One such example is the image of Paris. Although Paris between the wars had a major influence on the authors' lives at that time, McLain presents Paris in a different and more cheerful light than Fowler and Zelda do. This not only suggests that Hadley is the more optimistic and cheerful of the two American wives in

Paris but points to the fact that there is not one "factual" account of a time or a place. Although Hadley considers herself old-fashioned for cosmopolitan Paris, she falls in love with all the interesting people there and is truly happy with her life in Paris while accepting Hemingway as he is. Again, at this point, Hadley shows no *contamination* or *redemption* of any kind. Her narrative is predominantly of *coherent positive resolution*, self-mastery and achievement. Paris is the perfect setting of the scene for the beginning of their marriage, interesting people everywhere and anytime (see McLain:139).

Although Hadley's Paris at the beginning is exciting, at the end, her attitude changes a bit. After having lived there, they had become Paris, and Paris had become them, building everything together and then destroying it (see McLain:308).

What is interesting here to note is that the first-person narrator also takes the role of an omniscient narrator making references to what the future with Hemingway might turn out to be, which undermines the illusion of an authoritative autobiographical narrative and uncovers the hidden mechanisms of the postmodern writing in which the biographers have long ago lost the role of the truth-teller.

To complicate this subtle transition between fact and fiction, McLain also makes a point to include the different meetings the couple has within the actual artistic circles of Paris as an intrinsic part of the fictional narrative such as the meeting with such a major literary figure as Ezra Pound. Interweaving Pound's life with the story of the Hemingways uncovers some of the aspects of their friendship and thus becomes an example of *situatedness*. The fact that the events used to build the life narrative of Hemingway and his wife in Paris require all-the-time verification by the use of the factual, which becomes entangled with the fictional is part of the way biopreservation functions in biofictions. Such a mixture reveals also the literary and social motivations of the author's image building and makes the reader even more intrigued.

This claim is valid for the moment of Ernest meeting Gertrude Stein. They both represent the cultural myth of the artistic life in Paris and the whole idea of the Lost Generation. Stein's role is manifold. She is present at many decisive points in Ernest's life such as his establishment in artistic Paris and the beginning of his writing career. Their relationship is not just professional; they also become friends. In fact, she is the godmother of Hemingway's first child. She, together with Pound has a formative role in introducing Ernest into the literary world. All that can be interpreted as introducing the element of *communion* as part of the narrative identity McLain creates of that character. This particular side of Hadley is poignantly shown when she evaluates Hemingway's progress and achievement in light of serious inspection and criticism by established writers like Stein (See McLain:155).

This episode is a very good example of the blending process of biographical (knowing Stein's role as a literary critic) and fictional elements (the actual words Stein and Hemingway exchange) and involves projection of the specific traits of Hemingway's personality. This is also true about the selection of the many trips and adventures Hemingway makes across Europe as a journalist. His interview with Mussolini and his visits to Germany and Turkey attest to the way biofiction works making simple facts lead to an unexpected meaning and central inferences discarding obvious understandings. These facts turn into a powerful conversation between the spouses in McLain's book, where they discuss the state of events, calling Mussolini "a bully" and "a monster" (see McLain:175).

It is well documented that Hemingway's attitude towards Mussolini, from a mild dissatisfaction, grew into a vocal contempt. Hemingway and Mussolini had a few things in common: both were wounded in defense of Italy during WWI and both were newspapermen. According to Theriault, "Hemingway gleaned a softer side of Mussolini as he sat in his 'editorial chair' at the Milan's offices of *Popolo d'Italia* 'fondling the ears of his wolfhound pup.' Perhaps seeing a bit of himself in the Fascist leader's 'intellectual' face, and aware that Mussolini, too, had 'drifted into journalism' and was 'decorated for valor' in war, Hemingway opined that Mussolini, 'a patriot above all things', had been falsely accused by his opponents: 'He was a great surprise. He is not the monster he has been pictured.'" But Hemingway's disdain for Mussolini grew fast as Mussolini banned *A Farewell to Arms* in Italy, and he even called Il Duce "the biggest bluff in Europe" in his *Toronto Daily Star* article from January 27, 1923. These facts are fictionalized in the novel creating an image of a writer who freely plays with language and inserts his own words in the mouths of other people.

This aspect of Hemingway's past has led to another way of using intertextuality in the "imitation" of Hemingway's own journalistic writings. Hadley's account of their visit to Germany, another biopreservation sequence used by McLain, relies on a combination of the "story model" and the "information model". Thus, much as in all the other biopreservation sequences, Hadley assumes *agency*. The external facts and the world affairs of the day find again their place in the biopreservational sequences, building Hemingway's but especially Hadley's persona. She confidently discusses the unrests in Germany at the time (see McLain:195).

McLain inserts the journalistic style as one pertinent to Hadley, while it is well known that she had little to no interest in journalism or creative writing. Similarly, the story about Ernest going to Turkey suggests concrete historical-textual conjunctions. Their quarrel about him leaving for Turkey precedes a description of him in Turkey and a short affair with an Armenian girl. A third-person narrator narrates the period of his reporting on the Greco-Turkish War, the nights in Adrianople and the dark Armenian girl. In *The Paris Wife*, Hemingway is the hero who saves the girl from the hands of the British soldier (see McLain:119).

This is one of his adventures that is used to portray Hadley as a caring and forgiving wife. The insertion of a third-person narrator, in turn, emphasizes the two perspectives of the story, making the account of Hemingway's stay in Turkey impersonal and only Hadley's reaction to it, a personal one.

> I took up the scissors and cut his hair very close to his head and picked the rest of the lice out one by one, bringing the lamp over so I could see everything. Then I rubbed his body all over with cream and helped him into fresh clean sheets where he slept for twenty-four hours. [...] The breach between us had been terrible and the silence, too, but his time in Turkey had come to outshadow all of that.
>
> (McLain:211)

What is more, this event is intertextually recreated in the novel on the basis of Hemingway's own fictional account of his adventure during this assignment in "The Snows of Kilimanjaro". In the story, Harry, a writer dying of gangrene, and his wife Helen are on a safari in Africa. One of the many memories he recalls is his fight with a British soldier over an Armenian prostitute. He also recalls the war atrocities he saw then. Later he remembers returning to Paris where his then-wife inquires about a letter exchange between him and his first love in America, who is supposed to send her letters to his office in Paris while he is in Constantinople. This forms a narrative cluster built on both fictional and factual material and on the basis of the numerous intertextual ties that the narrative exploits creating a fictional image of Hadley and Hemingway's marital life that appears as true.

This whole string of narrative events closely follows some of the crucial events in Hemingway's life and Hadley's narrative processing of them. The event sequencing continues with the biofictional preservation of his third trip to Lausanne where they decide to go together but Hadley joins him later, on account of not feeling well. This trip is important for Ernest's contacts with colleagues and his writing career. At the same time, this is the part that uncovers the element of *sacrifice* on Hadley's part (see McLain:224).

On a biopreservation level, this particular story has echoes of Hemingway's complicated relationship with Anderson. As Josmall and Reynolds conclude, Ernest Hemingway was "eager to establish a reputation independent of Anderson", his one-time mentor. For that purpose, he wrote a satiric parody of Anderson's fiction called *The Torrents of Spring* (1926). Their mutual publisher Boni and Liveright refused to publish it and only later when the Scribner's published both the parody and the novel *The Sun Also Rises* did he manage to publicly distance himself from the older writer. Their dispute and mutual attacks were discussed in a series of letters. This episode becomes the basis of two stories, Hemingway's story, "The Killers", appeared in *Scribner's Magazine* and in *Men without Women* (1927), while Anderson's counterpart was a story called "The Fight". The stories reveal the authors' "deepest feelings about the personal and literary conflict between them" in terms of boxing. The matter seemed to have closed by 1927, "ending there at the point of Hemingway's rise and Anderson's virtual demise" (Josmall and Reynolds 2016). Therefore, the factual participants in this story serve to create intertextually multilayered images in the narrative sequences of *The Paris Wife*.

Continuing with the biopreservation sequences, McLain builds one of the crucial episodes in Hemingway and Hadley's relationship. It is here that another fact in Hemingway and Hadley's relationship becomes fictionalized. On her way to Lausanne, Hadley loses the valise with Hemingway's manuscripts, but Hemingway shows a complete understanding and not a single grudge against Hadley for having lost his manuscripts (see McLain:232).

This is not only a central episode in their relationship but also another rendition of Hadley's point of view. The Hemingway who emerges out of her narrative is calm and forgiving. This is an important moment in Hadley's narrative identity that in turn reaffirms Hemingway as a positive character.

The facts from their marriage continue to be the source of biopreservation sequences and narrative elements in this respect. Such an example is the moment when they are expecting their first child and plan Hemingway's career along the way. As presented in McLain's narrative, when it comes to having a baby, they are taking precautions for the time, but while in Switzerland, Hadley loses track of it. At the beginning, they are waiting for Ernest to make a good start, and a baby coming along is thought to make things more difficult. Nevertheless, the big start of his writing career was bound to happen. Within this biographical framework, McLain fictionally inserts the boost Hemingway needs to concentrate on his success as a writer. At the same time, this world-making biopreservation sequence throws Hadley's identity in *exploratory narrative processing* and a *coherent positive resolution* discarding any *sacrifice* on her side.

> They went off to ski alone while I did my best to find some peace. I put on some nice thick socks and my Alpine slippers and then curled up in a chair by the fire to read *The Beautiful and Damned.* 'Fitzgerald's a poet,' Shakespear had said when she recommended it, just before she and Pound left for several months in Italy. The writing was exquisite, I had to admit, but it was making me sad to read about Gloria and Anthony. They talked prettily and had nice things, but their lives were hollow. I didn't have the stomach for such a dire picture of marriage, not just now.
>
> (McLain:241)

This moment is an example of including fictional elements to reflect on "real" relations. Hadley's own account of her life situation is presented through a reader's identification with fictional characters, namely, those of Gloria and Antony in Fitzgerald's *The Beautiful and Damned.* This reference serves to help Hadley better understand her feelings about her relationship with Hemingway and to heal from the position of a victim marking a successful *exploratory narrative processing.*

Hadley's views on marriage are further revealed in her talk with Pound's wife over Pound's mistress (in a similar way Zelda refers to Pound's marital relations in *Z: A Novel of Zelda Fitzgerald*). In Hadley's understanding, her own familial bliss is in contrast with Pound's wife's open talk about her husband cheating on her. Pound's case is compared to Hemingway's infidelity. While

Pound's wife knows and openly speaks about her husband's mistress, Hadley would not be able to live in such a love triangle. The fictional conversation between the writers' wives about actual events emphasizes Hadley's position and identity. She clearly states that she cannot accept infidelity in marriage (see McLain:246).

The conversation between Hadley and Dorothy Shakespear, Pound's wife, reveals Hadley's intention not to turn her marital life into a detective story, as Dorothy seems to have done. McLain fictionally inserts the fact that Ezra Pound had a mistress and the fact that his wife knew that, making Hadley's own beliefs and attitudes towards marriage more realistic. For this purpose, the stories from the other trips of Hemingway and Hadley are also chronologically ordered in biopreservation sequences. By blurring the borderline between the factual and the fictional, their first trip to Pamplona, the birth of their baby in Canada and the return to Paris involve bold depictions of the couple's relationship and Hadley's understanding of herself. One example is the couple's welcoming of their child. Hemingway rushes dead worried to see his newborn son and wife and brave Hadley just says:

> Dear sweet Tiny. You can see I'm fine. Everything went smoothly, and come look at this fellow. Isn't he wonderful?
> (McLain:282)

What is even more interesting is that McLain uses the different biopreservation sequences that build the historiographic metafiction in an aesthetic way to achieve metonymical effects. The scene of seeing his baby echoes Hemingway's own fictional presentation of the birth of Henry's son in *A Farwell to Arms*:

> I sat in a chair at the foot of the bed. There was a nurse in the room. I got up and stood by the bed. It was dark in the room. Catherine put out her hand. 'Hello, darling,' she said. Her voice was very weak and tired. 'Hello, you sweet.' 'What sort of baby was it?' 'Sh—don't talk,' the nurse said. 'A boy. He's long and wide and dark.' 'Is he all right?' 'Yes,' I said. 'He's fine.' I saw the nurse look at me strangely. 'I'm awfully tired,' Catherine said. 'And I hurt like hell. Are you all right, darling?' 'I'm fine. Don't talk.' 'You were lovely to me. Oh, darling, I hurt dreadfully. What does he look like?' 'He looks like a skinned rabbit with a puckered-up old-man's face.' 'You must go out,' the nurse said. 'Madame Henry must not talk.'
> (Hemingway 1929:278)

In *A Farewell to Arms*, however, the ending of the story is tragic, where both the mother and the baby die. The novel was published the year following his second son's birth and draws on the difficult labor Pauline, his second wife, had. In McLain's book, the metonymical over-layering of this story goes back to the birth of Hemingway's first son and in contrast with the previous fictional and factual versions, it fictionally recreates a happy scene of the young parents with their newly born son.

Since historiographic metafiction is characterized by the re-ordering of events and re-shaping of historical figures, in the attempt to convey an idea of truthfulness, McLain has left some of the events and figures basically unchanged. Such is the case with the figure of John Dos Passos in the novel. His historical figure is reestablished as a successful writer who actively participates in the artistic circles of Paris. "John Dos Passos, whom Ernest had met just after he began working for the Red Cross in Italy, was back in Paris, riding the wave of his literary success and always ready for a good time" (McLain:312). This is only little different from the known facts already established by the biographers.

On the other hand, Ernest's meeting Lady Twysden and Hadley's meeting Pauline at Kitty's are used differently, using the factual to represent the starting points of the changes that follow in their lives. Thus, the literary rendition of these events is a challenge to the genre structure since what we have is the biographical blending effortlessly with fiction leading to *world making/world disrupting*. We know that the two women met in real life, but the choice of a first-person narrative makes the meeting between them more effective when rendered through the eyes of the wife. In that way, Hadley's narrative identity is successfully established. The above biopreservation sequences lead to Hadley's *communion* and a *coherent positive resolution*. Once again, she does not see herself as a victim in her divorce with Hemingway.

We will never know whether these were the exact feelings of Hadley, who describes Pauline as the more fashionable, free-spirited young woman (see McLain:330). Her perfect clothes, shoes and style are contrasted with Hadley's shabby dressing despite the fact that they both came from the Midwest and would seem to have a similar style of dressing. McLain, however, prefers to see them as strikingly different, so that she could build a more convincing narrative identity for her protagonist, Hadley.

The central part in the novel is meeting the Fitzgeralds and the description of the nature of their friendship and their opinion of each other. Once uncovered and rendered fictionally, the facts assume a different power. Unlike Fowler, McLain does not develop this biopreservation sequence in order to uncover the reason behind the authors' frenemy. She dismisses it as unimportant for Hadley's narrative identity. Instead, Hadley narrates the story in retrospect, from the point of view of a divorced though happy woman who seems to feel sorry for the Fitzgeralds and their failures:

> On a night in early May, Ernest and I were having a night out on our own at the Dingo when Scott Fitzgerald came over from the bar and introduced himself to us. 'You're Hemingway,' Fitzgerald said. 'Ford showed me a story of yours a few weeks back and I said, 'Well there it is, isn't it? He's the real article.' 'I'm sorry I haven't read any of your books,' Ernest said.
> (McLain:343)

In this central scene, the factual and fictional accounts widely differ as both are interwoven to create a unique set of fictional relations based on real characters. The actual meeting between the two lifelong friends did happen in the Dingo, but neither Hadley nor Zelda were present at the meeting. In McLain's narrative only Hadley, Hemingway and Fitzgerald are present at the meeting and Fitzgerald introduces himself to the American couple. In Fowler's narrative as seen before, it is the other way around, i.e. Hadley is the one missing at the meeting, and Ezra Pound is the one who introduces the two authors. Hemingway tells the story of their meeting in the chapter called "F. Scott Fitzgerald" in *A Moveable Feast*:

> The first time I ever met Scott Fitzgerald a very strange thing happened. Many strange things happened with Scott but this one I was never able to forget. He had come into the Dingo bar in the rue Delambre where I was sitting with some completely worthless characters, had introduced himself and introduced a tall, pleasant man who was with him as Dunc Chaplin, the famous pitcher. I had not followed Princeton baseball and had never heard of Dunc Chaplin but he was extraordinarily nice, unworried, relaxed and friendly and I much preferred him to Scott.
> (Hemingway 1964:149)

In McLain's narrative, Hemingway and Hadley first meet Zelda when Fitzgerald asks them to a dinner in their apartment, which is another opposite biopreservation sequence and opposite world-making from the one presented in Fowler's book, relying on intertextual parody. McLain builds the image of F. Scott Fitzgerald as a writer who greatly admires Hemingway and would very much like to leave a good impression on him while being torn by his wife's demands and his unstable writing endeavors. Hemingway and Hadley on the other hand, stand for the more stable couple of the two. Fitzgerald, for example, is the confused man desperately in love with Zelda.

'That's all right. I'm not sure I write them anymore. Since my wife and I have come to Paris it's been a thousand parties and no work at all.' Ernest squinted at him through the dim light. 'You can't finish anything that way.' 'Don't I know it? But Zelda loves to dance. You should meet her. She's spectacular.' His eyes turned to the dance floor where several couples were in the midst of a sinuous-looking tango. 'I do have a novel just out, *The Great Gatsby.*' 'I'll look for it,' Ernest said. 'How are you holding up, waiting for the notices?' 'That's not so difficult for me. Not near as tricky as getting it down in the first place. And once I have it all, I can't seem to move on. Like this Gatsby. I know him so well, it's as if he's my child. He's dead and I'm still worried about him. Isn't that funny?'

(McLain:343)

Much in the same way as with the episode of Hemingway–Fitzgerald meeting, McLain creates intertextual ties throughout the whole novel. As seen above, these include preservation of factual, documentary and literary information. The party of the "Lost Generation" traveling to Pamplona that serves as the material of *The Sun Also Rises* is duly referred to in McLain's biofiction by a series of intertextual references. Hemingway's third trip to Pamplona in June 1925 involved, in addition to Hadley, his Michigan friend Bill Smith, Donald Ogden Stewart, the recently divorced Lady Duff Twysden, her lover Pat Guthrie and Harold Loeb. The company meets the young matador Cayetano Ordonez. Hemingway's *The Sun Also Rises* turns Hemingway into Jake Barnes, Lady Twysden is Lady Brett Ashely, Bill Smith and Donald Ogden Stewart together form the character of Bill Gorton, Pat Guthrie is Mike Campbell and Harold Loeb is Robert Cohn, while Ordonez becomes Romero. This circle of real friends becomes fictionalized for a second time in McLain's book as a specific element of world-making and situatedness. Her painting of the group involved initial connection between Ernest and Duff in Paris but she goes on to say "something had come to change it and that something was Harold" (McLain:348).

Interestingly, Hadley is not included in the list of *The Sun Also Rises* characters. However, it is a known fact that relations in the group become intense, complicated and chaotic. Hadley's fictional account in *The Paris Wife* gives yet another interpretation of these relationships in addition to the factual account in Hemingway's biography (see Baker 1972) and the fictional one in his novel.

> When he pulled away, his eyes were moist and questioning. 'I don't suppose you love me, too, just a little?' 'I wish I did. It might balance things out.' I put my arms around his [Donald's] neck and held him close for a moment, feeling the sadness and confusion, all mixed up together in him. 'This place has us all going crazy.'
>
> (McLain:355)

This is one of the most striking differences between the factual account of the events and its novelistic portrayal in *The Sun Also Rises* and *The Paris Wife*. The author introduces a close moment between Hadley and Donald as part of the group in Pamplona as a reaction to Hemingway's flirting with Lady Twysden. In Diliberto's biography, Hadley is presented as the one having the least fun, seeming "gloomy" while Donald is the one to notice Hadley's sadness and who tries to cheer her up. This presentation coincides with the biographer's presentation of Donald Stewart as a wonderful person, a witty and good-spirited man. Donald met Beatrice Aimes in Paris the same year as the Pamplona trip and the couple married in 1926.

In McLain's narrative, the people on the Pamplona trip are presented as an entangled mixture of representatives of the Lost Generation, drunk and lost in the seemingly enjoyable time. Hadley recognizes the futility of this gathering underlining Hemingway's concept of the Lost Generation as presented in *The Sun Also Rises*. The role of the matador is also preserved in Hadley's story to serve the change of perspective. In McLain's book, the matador slices off the ear of the bull and gives it to Hadley as a present (McLain:368), again to underline Hadley's identity, understanding and position against all the events taking place.

In this episode, McLain changes the perspective from a fictional presentation to retelling the factual account of the story as given in

Hemingway's biography (Baker 1972) in which Hadley is given the special gift by the matador. In *The Sun Also Rises*, Lady Twysden is given the honor to possess the ear cut from the bull. In this way, McLain intertextually gives Hadley a place in the story of *The Sun Also Rises*, a story she is left out of. As a result, this scene further supports Hadley's *coherent positive resolution*.

Another biopreservation sequence is formed based on their return to Paris where Pauline introduces them to the Murphys. This couple plays an important role in the social lives of both the Hemingways and the Fitzgeralds. The friendship with Pauline continues and they all go to Austria for skiing, Pauline being delighted to join them. Pauline and Hemingway's getting together is introduced by a third-person narrator marking the element of *world disrupting*. McLain's use of another voice in the narration again gives a balance to some points and clears the perspectives to the situation indirectly signaling *agency* amid *contamination*. These interchanging narrative combinations are also an attempt by McLain to match the tone of Hemingway's *A Movable Feast* in which he fondly remembers his first wife where he says: "I wish I had died before I ever loved anyone but her...". McLain describes this situation using an omniscient narrator: "He loved them both and that's where the pain came in" (McLain:424).

The third-person narrator, although impartial, tells the story from Hemingway's point of view. According to Hotchner, Hemingway did love them both and wanted to keep them both if that was possible. In a conversation with Fitzgerald, he confesses: "But now I love them both. May bring me bad luck but I hope not. Hope we can go along like this" (Hotchner 2015:40). The story of Pound's infidelity is intertextually inserted here to level Hemingway's opinion and fictionally render it as his.

Switching back to the first-person narrator gives McLain the opportunity to side with Hadley. Hadley confronts Hemingway on the matter while the love triangle becomes even more complicated.

> Zelda and Ernest had never liked each other. He thought she had too much power over Scott, that she was a destructive force and probably half mad to boot. She thought he was a phony, putting on macho airs to hide an effeminate center. 'I think you're in love with my husband,' she said to Ernest one night when we were down at the beach and everyone had had too much to drink.
>
> (McLain:453)

These renditions attest to the plurality of meanings and interpretations arising from the ideas at work. While Zelda's character is given one meaning in *Z: A Novel of Zelda Fitzgerald*, in *The Paris Wife*, the narrator seems to take Ernest's side in the argument, dismissing Zelda as an unstable and unserious person. Zelda's character is a typical example of postmodern fictional creation. The Fitzgeralds, the Murphys and the rest of their Paris friends get involved in the marital problems of the couple. McLain inserts Zelda's opinion on Sara and Murphy's marriage, her and Ernest's short argument, but also her discussion with Hadley on the Pauline matter.

Yet another biopreservation sequence is formed around the end of Hemingway's marriage. This part represents a culmination of Hadley's strength and character building. She openly talks about her realizing Hemingway's and Pauline's affair, while they all stayed at a hotel on the coastline, all starting to happen in front of her eyes (see McLain:464).

Hemingway's close personal friend, A. E. Hotchner, published several books about Hemingway's life. In 2015, he published *Hemingway in Love: His Own Story* including their conversations and Hemingway's personal confessions about his life and marriages. The above quote is Hadley's fictional confession about the deterioration of their marriage. In Hotchner's book, Hemingway makes a similar confession:

> Pauline moved into a room next to ours and right away she took charge. Brought the morning coffee and croissants to our room, sat on the edge of my side of the bed while we three shared our petit dejuner.
> (Hotchner 2015:37)

This confession, however, was published after McLain's book.

This is the time when Hadley's marriage slowly falls apart in front of her eyes. On their return to Paris, the end of their marriage was becoming a fact. Nevertheless, the factual moment of the "hundred-day" agreement is placed as a conclusive point in the novel. It is known from Hemingway's biographies that Hadley gave Hemingway a one-hundred-day period in which he was not supposed to meet Pauline. If after this period, he still wanted to be with Pauline she would give him a divorce. Hemingway had a hard time getting through this crisis. He did not see Pauline but was writing to her. McLain portrays this period by employing a third-person narrator: "He still loved Hadley afterward" (McLain:505) but "Pauline was his future" (McLain:505), concluding that Hemingway himself was never going to trust anyone again.

To further emphasize the different points of view, McLain makes use of the epistolary genre to highlight the dramatic ending. It is a known fact that they did settle the end of their marriage through letters, though the letters McLain inserts are fictional accounts of what Hadley might have said in response to Hemingway's letters. According to Hadley's biographer, Gioia Diliberto,

> Ernest kept Hadley's love letters all his life. His fourth wife, Mary, sent them back to Hadley after his suicide in 1961 and Hadley kept them for another eighteen years. After her death in 1979, Jack Hemingway found them stuffed into a shoe box in her Florida apartment. [...] Most of Ernest's letters though did not survive. Hadley burnt them one day after their marriage collapsed, one of the few outward signs of her rage and sorrow.
> (Diliberto 2011: preface)

According to Hotchner, after the divorce, Hadley gave Hemingway back the letters he wrote to her. "Tatie" is Hemingway's pet name for Hadley and in *The Paris Wife*, Hadley uses it to refer to Hemingway in her letters. In the heartbreaking fictional letter, Hadley parts with Hemingway and braves out trying to cope with her extreme pain in the best possible way: "I can't quarrel with you anymore and I can't see you much either, because it hurts too much. We'll always be friends – delicate friends, and I'll love you 'til I die, you know. Ever yours, the Cat" (McLain:510).

The heartbreak of their relationship is poignantly evident in their personal letters more than anywhere else. The letters continue to show Hemingway in an amicable, sympathetic way, her exploratory narrative processing and meaning-making of a difficult situation. The factual moment of the one-hundred-day ultimatum is fictionally inserted into Hadley's letters to Hemingway. According to Hotchner, both Hemingway and Hadley suffered terribly during this period, Hemingway even said that he considered killing himself: "Just a disappearance. It would absolve Pauline of sin, Hadley would avoid having to divorce me, and Bumby would be told that angels came to get his papa" (Hotchner 2015:91). Nevertheless, according to Hotchner's account, the agony ended after just 75 days when Hadley wrote that she could no longer wait and she was granting him divorce. In Hotchner's book, Hemingway talks about how Hadley's letter made him feel:

> My numbness slowly gave way to the reality of her letter. I suppose that down deep I had been unrealistically hoping that when the hundred days were up Hadley would decide to go along to keep both of them in my life [...] But Hadley's terse, stark letter, giving up on me made me feel her pain, her exclusion, the loss I had inflicted on her, and my thoughts became very concerned about my soul.
>
> (Hotchner 2015: 108)

The story ends with their last conversation, in 1961, the year of Hemingway's death, another evidence of the heartbreak they both endured. This fictional conversation underlines the connection between the two and makes the end of their life together more dramatic.

> 'You're everywhere in the book,' he said, and his voice dipped. He was working hard to stay cheerful, but I knew he was sad and low and haunted. 'It's been something, writing that time and living it all again. Tell me, do you think we wanted too much from each other?'
>
> (McLain: Epilogue)

Hemingway did write to Hadley later in life. According to Hotchner, he met Hadley only once again in his life, after his divorce from Pauline, by chance in Paris. After he saw her get out of taxi, he approached her and, she put her arms around him. After they sat to have a drink and while telling her he would always love her, they separated as he said: "I'll spend the rest of my life looking for you. Good-bye Tatie. The light changed to green. Hadley turned and kissed me, a meaningful kiss; then she crossed the street and I watched her go, that familiar, graceful walk" (Hotchner 2015:151). In contrast, Allie Baker (2010) states that the last time Hadley and her second husband Paul met Hemingway was in 1939 in Wyoming and the last time they spoke, to ask about her memories of Paris, was the same year Hemingway commits suicide.

Another aspect of the image building is the fact that Hadley's name appears 27 times in *A Moveable Feast*, Pauline's nine, Mary Hemingway's eight times and Martha Gellhorn's name does not appear at all in the memoir. Obviously, Hadley is the wife that stayed on Hemingway's mind. McLain uses this explicit presence of Hadley in Hemingway's thoughts towards the end of his life to create the fictional image of Hemingway who shows genuine affection for Hadley and their times together. She is portrayed not as the first to be left out, but as the only one who had really stayed in his life. Hemingway's emotional outbreak in *A Moveable Feast* points to this idea. In McLain's novel, he has to make his goodbye with Hadley before he dies as he did by writing the material about their life together in *A Moveable Feast*. Paula McLain's ending of the book is in line with Allie Baker's list of the events in Hadley's life which appeared before *The Paris Wife* was published while Hotchner's book *Hemingway in Love: His Own Story* was published in 2015, three years after the publication of *The Paris Wife*. The underlying idea, therefore, is to confirm Hadley's identity marked by *positive coherent resolution* as the leading element of her personal story.

There are, of course, other biopreservation sequences that can be created in an attempt to re-tell Hemingway's life and they can render various textual meanings. One such specific instance linked to Pauline and the love triangle between her, Hemingway and Hadley and Hemingway's divorce from Hadley and marriage to Pauline in the same year can be traced in the "sequel" of *The Paris Wife*, Robuck's *Hemingway's Girl*, which deals with another love triangle involving Hemingway, Pauline and a young American-Cuban girl from the Florida Keys.

More precisely, the refracted images occur as a result of the narrative biopreservation of three different love triangles, Hemingway playing central part in all of them. The first one between Mariella, Hemingway and Gavin is used to illuminate Hemingway's figure as a rich successful author, extremely charismatic, but also married for the second time, as opposed to Gavin – a down-to-earth, honest ex-soldier. Despite their different socio-economic status, they are very similar, and Mariella's attraction is used to emphasize their contrasting figures. Gavin, like Hemingway, took part in WWI, enjoys boxing but he lacks Hemingway's literary fame. Robuck puts Hemingway's lady's man figure as an extravagant personality in the shade of his counterpart, Gavin.

The other love triangle parodically produces yet another meaning to contrast previous events in the author's life. Pauline, a woman known to have stolen Hemingway from his first wife, becomes insecure at the backdrop of the Hemingway–Pauline–Hadley triangle. Both Hemingway and Pauline are put to a test. It is a question of how they would each react in the appearance of another woman. This leads to the third love triangle, the one between Pauline, Hemingway and their friend Jane. By means of intertextuality Robuck juxtaposes different facets of the era: the indulgent extravagance of the Hemingways, in contrast to the hardships of WWI veterans, is as fascinating as it is heartbreaking. She generates meaning from the brute events by spicing up a historical event. The household drama is coupled with the desolate plight of the veterans. A reference is made to the Labor Day Hurricane in 1935 and the veterans' situation during the Depression of the 1930s, for which Hemingway wrote and published the article "Who Murdered the Vets?" It was published on September 17, 1935, a few weeks after the Florida Hurricane as a first-hand report and a personal account. In the article, Hemingway asks, "Whom did they annoy and to whom was their possible presences a political danger? Who sent them down the Florida Keys and left them there in the hurricane months?" (Murphy 1989: 112).

As has already been discussed, the postmodern biofiction often takes the form of a detective story. Both Robuck and McLain adopt this style. As part of the genre bending, it appears McLain wants her readers to believe that this is not another mystery to solve but a factual account of Hadley and Hemingway's lives. Here Hadley, at the very beginning of the book, tells the story about the end of her marital bliss, giving an implicit idea about the main perpetrator in this regard, Pauline. The audience recognizes and delights in such references. Although they know the real-life figures of the characters and how the story ends, such storytelling provides the thrill of getting to participate in their lives. Hadley's friend Kate, John Dos Passos, the Fitzgeralds, the Murphys, Gertrude Stein, Pauline, their families and friends on both sides of the Atlantic all play their part in the biopreservation sequences to emphasize the mystery of the biographical figures of Hemingway and Hadley in particular.

On the other hand, Robuck's images of the biographees are mainly illustrated through the love triangles.

> 'I don't know how I've become so helpless,' said Pauline. Mariella thought it sounded [more] like an address to the universe than a conversation starter, so she stayed quiet. 'It's because of how we started, me and Papa,' said Pauline. She now looked at Mariella, directly addressing her. 'And how's that?' asked Mariella – fully aware of how that was. 'He was married to Hadley when we fell in love,' she said. 'And now I'll always worry that he'll fall in love with another once he's tired of me. You're lucky to have your soldier, Mariella.' 'You've seen them,' said Pauline. 'Do you think he loves Jane?'
>
> (Robuck:217)

The fact that Pauline became Hemingway's second wife as a result of her winning in a love triangle, is parodically used here to mirror her image in two other triangles.

The presence of Mariella and Jane around Hemingway throws Pauline into despair which is the opposite of the Paris Pauline in McLain's book. Robuck later introduces the character of Jane as one of the members of the party at Bimini as a counterpart of Pauline joining Hadley and Hemingway on their trips to Austria and the French Riviera. The friendships of the Hemingways with other people are intertextually used for that purpose. According to Hotchner, Hemingway wanted to spend his evenings with a "beautiful twenty-two-year-old beauty named Jane Mason". She was married but also started an affair with Hemingway.

> 'Did Pauline know about her?' I asked. Made sure she did. Unlike hiding my affair with Pauline from Hadley, I wanted to know what was going on with Jane. I wrote Pauline all about Jane, even sent her a photo of Jane and me on the *Anita*. 'You were giving her plenty of ammunition for a divorce?' 'It was time. But Pauline would not make the same mistake as Hadley. No hundred days.'
>
> (Hotchner 2015:134)

The factual presence of Jane Mason in Hemingway's life intertextually surfaced in the image of the third person in the love triangle. Her youth is embodied in the image of Mariella, but also in the fictional character of Jane.

The other love triangle, not involving Pauline mirrors both the image of Hemingway as a macho figure and his interest in boxing.

> 'Winner takes all,' said the yachtsman, dropping in twenty. 'One round, knockout Papa.' 'When is the fight?' asked Mariella.
> 'Tomorrow morning. Nine o'clock,' said Papa. 'At the dock where you came in.'
> Gavin nodded soberly and took a swig of his drink.
> 'I'll go easy on your face,' said Papa. 'Don't worry about that.' said Gavin. 'Damage is done there.'
>
> (Robuck:220)

Robuck makes a significant point of challenging Hemingway's image as a supreme boxer. She combines the dismantling of his winning image in sport with his winning image with women. Hemingway ends up losing both the match and Mariella to Gavin.

The epistolary aspect of the end of the story embodies truth and honesty and thus metafictionally functions as a parodical pastiche. Both Fowler and McLain use the letter exchange between Fitzgerald and Hemingway and their family and friends in the same way in their biofictions. In the many letters Robuck introduces, there is one letter where Hemingway refers to Fitzgerald, after his death as another example of refracted images:

> Still recovering from the Spanish Civil War. For the first time I felt like I was getting old for this shit. I'm hoping the Finca will restore me while I grieve humanity and some old friends I lost, most notably, F. Scott. When I got word that he died of a heart attack earlier this month I nearly had my own. I didn't expect to outlive him. Thinking of him makes me sad and a little bit angry. With more discipline, a better tolerance and no Zelda he could have been a great man. But all of that was under his control (barring the tolerance issue), so I shouldn't pity him. And who am I to pass judgment on others on the subject of drinking or women?
>
> (Robuck:234)

The letter offers yet another image of the Fitzgerald–Hemingway friendship as a sequence to those in Fowler's and McLain's books. It intertextually inserts Hemingway's claim that Zelda was the reason for Fitzgerald's problems: "I did not know Zelda yet, and so I did not know the terrible odds that were against him. But we were to find that out soon enough" (Hemingway 2010: 176). He even called her "crazy". In *A Moveable Feast*, Hemingway makes a point to deride his friend Fitzgerald as a weak drunk:

> Scott ate very little and sipped at one glass of the wine. He passed out at the table with his head on his hands. It was natural and there was no theater about it and it even looked as though he were careful not to spill nor break things. The waiter and I got him up to his room and laid him on the bed and I undressed him to his underwear, hung his clothes up, and then stripped the covers off the bed and spread them over him. I opened the window and saw it was clear outside and left the window open.
>
> (Hemingway 2010: 174)

He goes on to feel pity for Fitzgerald: "'Isn't Scott happy at all?' 'Maybe. Poor man.' 'I learned one thing.' 'What?' 'Never to go on trips with anyone you do not love.' 'Isn't that fine?'" (Hemingway 2010:174). This idea was reflected in Robuck's letter in which Hemingway is genuinely sorry for the loss of his friend, but also underlines that he does not pity him. In addition, he seems to no longer believe that he is better than Fitzgerald when it comes to women and drinking.

Robuck uses another letter to establish still more intertextual ties. Hemingway's prize-winning *The Old Man and the Sea* is mentioned in another letter he sends to Mariella.

> I told you I would never use you. But I did. It was in *The Old Man and the Sea* – the only thing I've ever been really proud of. It was the truest writing I've ever done. Santiago was the best man I ever wrote and the fish and the hunt was the best hunt. No doubt you think you are the boy. You are like the boy because you are good to me and because I always wished you were with me.
>
> (Robuck:320)

The letter metafictionally refers to the story in *The Old Man and the Sea* and through the voice of Hemingway parodically establishes Mariella as the inspiration for the character in the boy of the book. In addition, the fact that this particular work brought Hemingway both the Pulitzer Prize for Literature in 1953 and The Nobel Prize for Literature a year later is used as a source for Hemingway's special pride in it as expressed in the letter.

The above comparative analysis leads to the conclusion that biopreservation builds the characters and the meaning-making of the narrative identity of the protagonists by exhibiting a unique genre play. In line with these narratives also falls the real-life memoir of Hemingway's third wife, Martha Gellhorn.

Storytelling entails telling and enacting as many kinds of stories in social life as there are social situations within which to tell and enact them. Each performance can be imagined as text to be deconstructed to reveal the shifting dynamics involved. Martha Gellhorn, Hemingway's third wife is considered one of the greatest journalists of the century and the one to truly match Hemingway in the profession. His first two wives, Hadley and Pauline did not pursue writing careers, although Pauline was a Vogue journalist and a graduate from a prestigious University of Missouri School of

Journalism, she left only a few poems and many letters. The only biography about Pauline, *Unbelievable Happiness and Final Sorrow: The Hemingway–Pfeiffer Marriage* by Ruth Hawkins was published in 2012. The book reveals many unknown facts about Pauline and her role as Hemingway's wife. Hemingway's fourth wife, Mary Welsh did write a biography. Entitled *How It Was*, it is an example of a biographical story written in the first person, but it is a biography that wants to present the events realistically in the traditional way, as the title suggests.

Martha Gellhorn's personal memoir on the other hand is an example of the multi-layering of personalities and events. Her story opens up the discussion about yet another Hemingway as presented in a personal narrative. Gellhorn had a never-ending lust for traveling and covering events from every corner of the world through wars and riots. Hemingway gets his due characterization in her *Travels with Myself and Another: A Memoir*, which illustrates her personal understanding of her life and thereby colors Hemingway's character in a different light. To begin with, Hemingway is the implicit "another" from the title of the book, and the UC (or unwilling companion) from the story of their way to China. Hemingway is an indispensable character, although unacknowledged, and their story together adds to the spirit of the war and the travel across the Pacific. "All I had to do was get to China. On this super horror journey, I wheedled an Unwilling Companion, hereinafter referred to as UC, into going where he had no wish to go" (Gellhorn 1978:20). Gellhorn's personal account is still another example of narrative identity that affirms the position of a *positive coherent resolution*, similarly to the fictional account of Hadley Richardson.

In this story, Hemingway as the Unwilling Companion is not even mentioned by his real name. His image is directly inflected to the narrative identity of Gellhorn's narrator in the first person.

> Trays crashed off our laps, bottles spilled; the ship proceeded with the motion of a dolphin, lovely in a dolphin and vile in a ship. UC muttered a lot; why had nobody warned us, if he had known the Pacific was this kind of ocean he would never have set a foot on it, a man should stick with the waters he knew, as a matter of fact he knew many lakes and rivers too and look at it in any way you want, M, this is a bad sign.
> (Gellhorn 1978:20)

The memoir was published in 1978, after Hemingway's death. Her understanding is that without him, she probably would not have survived.

> In China, water is like justice in that it has to be boiled and seen to be boiled; UC supervised this. UC also checked the quinine intake, which I'd have forgotten or muddled. He arranged extra shots against all the available diseases. By myself I'd have wrung my hands and groaned and caught every germ and ended up dead.
> (Gellhorn 1978: 33)

Another point is the lack of intimate expressions between the two. Gellhorn's not naming Hemingway by his own name is the first step in her parodic rendition of the fissure between them. He is the UC (unwilling companion) who is dragged around but manages to find his own amusements alluding to his interest in different people and their stories. Gellhorn intertextually inserts the fact that Hemingway loved fishing and using that for narratively clustering the events in China, she forms new images of Hemingway.

> UC had finished a long piece of work before we left the US and if I hadn't coaxed him to China he would have been loafing somewhere probably with a fishing rod.
> (Gellhorn 1978: 29)

Gellhorn, like Zelda in *Save Me the Waltz* does not speak about her husband overtly, and in this story, one would not know that it is Hemingway that is referred to, if it were not known that Gellhorn was his wife. Hemingway's character arises from the social relationships the couple forms, the setting, as well as the selectivity of what should be put in the story. She concludes the story of her incredible journey with the following reference to Hemingway:

> I wanted to praise UC for his generosity, above and beyond the call of duty, in coming to China, his forbearance in not murdering me, his jokes and let him know that I grieved for his time wasted on a season in hell. My brain was boiled; I couldn't form sentences. With tears in my eyes I touched his shoulders and said, 'Thank you'. He wrenched away, shouting: 'Take your filthy dirty hand off me!' We looked at each other in shocked

silence. Were these to be parting words between us after all the shared horrors of a super horror journey? Then we rolled on the marble floor laughing in our separate pools of sweat.

(Gellhorn 1978: 63)

This Hemingway in Gellhorn's story about China is a unique image of the American author. He is presented as a reluctant but still supportive husband in their marriage, but hardly the alfa man in his previous marriages. His sense of humor and robust character intertextually remain in the story but form a completely different picture of him from that in *The Paris Wife* or *Hemingway's Girl*, for example. Gellhorn herself always assumes *agency* and renders a *coherent positive resolution*.

These three different literary renditions of familiar plots and characters attest to the competitive interplay between life-writing and fiction. The view of the biofictions as meaning makers completes the new genre where it offers incompleteness or where it both constructs and deconstructs socio-cultural contexts, which is the essence of biopreservation. This process of biofictional preservation shows clearly how postmodern literary textual meaning is derived and acknowledges the deconstructive and heuristic potential of fiction. For the writer of biofictions this means that a fictional or emphatic/sympathetic approach to the subject involves playing with factual and fictional material to produce plausible interpretation of a person's life. Being written in the first person, *The Paris Wife* self-reflexively comments, de-bunks and demystifies Hemingway's figure and the complete picture of the artistic life in Paris. McLain builds Hadley's narrative identity and portrays a unique Hemingway as a "by-product". At the same time, *Hemingway's Girl* is another unique rendition of Hemingway's deconstructed figure as a husband and a lover. Gellhorn's memoir also cannot do without its specific narrative framing of her husband. All three narratives strikingly deploy Hemingway's reproduced images, whose immediacy the readers are made to feel by following all three personal accounts. The biopreservation sequences, therefore, tighten the net of Hemingway's life and produce images of him and the women around him that create alternative life stories for their readers. They also help to create fluctuating narrative identities that subvert and deconstruct the established ones.

Conclusion

As seen above, the field of life-writing lacks its own specific theory, most specifically on a textual level, that could serve as a basic tool in all kinds of different analytical accounts. We also saw how complex and entangled the field is in that sense. Therefore, this study offers responses to the questions about the interplay of fact and fiction and the resulting creation of a new hybrid genre. In particular, it gives explanations about the process of textual composition of framing and articulating the lived experience of famous literary figures, by proposing the theory of life-writing intertextuality called biopreservation.

In the first part, the study outlines the theoretical foundations of the research. It touches upon the concept of genre, genre play and narrative analysis within the postmodern paradigm. More importantly, the study postulates the theoretical background for the enterprise of biofiction. It shows that the fictional and auto/biographical narrative is an artfully contrived narrative practice. As such, this practice is investigated in terms of generic conventions, narrative elements, narrative identity and textual construction. These concepts prove to be complementary and equally indispensable in illustrating the construction of the genre.

Such theoretical background accommodates an unencumbered approach to life-writing textuality in the form of biopreservation. The line of my argument begins with the establishment of the narrative elements as constitutive parts of the story conceived in the form of a fictional auto/biography. The closer inspection comes with the narrative sequences that, in essence, generate the narrative elements. In this way, the specific textuality of life-writing genre play is established.

The dual nature of the sequences as both factual and fictional is the turning point in demystifying the narrative practice in life-writing genre play. The sequences imbue the narrative elements with meaning whose reverberating effect establishes the narrative identities of the biographees. The disclosure of the narrative elements in the biofictions establishes the fictional narrative flow of Zelda and Hadley's self-discoveries. This inevitably puts them in opposition to the established figures of their husbands. In addition, the comparison of these narrative developments with the ones in the fictional narratives again confirms the viability of the theoretical and analytical approaches.

Therese Ann Fowler's biofiction *Z: A Novel of Zelda Fitzgerald* signals its hybrid nature from the very beginning. The title tells us that it is a novel that recounts the life of Zelda Fitzgerald. The initial letter of her name somewhat suggests mystery to be unraveled in the life narrative. It also alludes to possible pinpointing of her image and status as Fitzgerald's wife. The biopreservation sequences in the text tackle the themes of the Fitzgeralds' marriage and their individual personal and professional endeavors. In many instances, the "bio" elements differ from Zelda's own narrative in *Save Me the Waltz*, which further emphasizes the unique narrative and the image building.

The first-person narrative in Fowler's book attests to Zelda's narrative identity as one of gradual progression, reaching the point of personal and forgiving confession. In this way, she weighs both hers and Fitzgerald's flaws as illustrated in crucial points of their lives. The tone is regretful and yet, one of making peace with both Fitzgerald and her past.

Fitzgerald's character is presented as one of a loving but jealous and awkwardly insecure husband. She often blames that for their misfortunes. Towards the end of the story, her tone changes and she feels sorry for Fitzgerald. The novel tackles another important segment of their lives, i.e. the meeting with Ernest Hemingway. He is presented in the most negative context, his detrimental influence as the worst thing that ever happened to Fitzgerald. He is portrayed as a show-off and manipulative "friend" who spreads gossips about her and Fitzgerald. Hadley, on the other hand, is not the exact down-to-earth woman who is about to divorce Hemingway, as presented in *The Paris Wife*. Here she is rather the person people feel sorry for, especially Zelda, for having married Hemingway.

In a similar way, it is the title of McLain's book, *The Paris Wife*, that right away suggests a genre mixing, not a biography but about somebody's life as a married woman in Paris, i.e. a narrative based on biographical facts. As it has been discussed, it is about a real historical figure, Hadley Richardson, who, as the main protagonist,

Conclusion 99

narrates the book. At times, there is also third-person narrative, to give a balanced account on certain issues between the couples. For much of the narrative, Hadley seems to be the moral winner in their marital fights. The characters of Zelda and Fitzgerald are parodically presented with a subtle mocking effect. There seems to be nothing majestic about the Fitzgeralds' story while Hemingway remains in the limelight of the Paris ex-patriate circle.

Hemingway and Pauline get another treatment by the fictional character of Mariella in Erica Robuck's *Hemingway's Girl*. Introducing a seemingly "neutral" narrator, Robuck portrays Hemingway in his best years in America. The biopreservation sequences underline his image as a father, an established writer and more reasonable in his marriage with Pauline. Pauline, on the other hand, is nothing like the self-confident modern American woman in Paris. She is rather an insecure wife slowly failing Hemingway.

This study has explored the phenomena of genre blending in life-writing. Applying the concept of biopreservation as an intertextual subtype the analysis offers a better understanding of the processes of this type of literary writing. Furthermore, this concept significantly increases the appeal of the genre and the reader's interest because it involves curiosity and surprise as to how the experiment of biopreservation turned out.

The above study shows that any auto/biographical material can be handled differently by different authors and more so when it comes to a narrative, subject to a life-writing genre play. Admittedly, biopreservation can adopt some properties pertaining to the social and cultural periods of its creation, but its essential form remains unchanged. In fictional auto/biographical writing, the established narrative identities of the narrator/protagonist/biographee enable the evaluation of the purpose and the success of the fictional narrative. Communicating a unique understanding and meaning seems to be the ultimate goal of this narrative practice. Finally, this study concludes that biopreservation as inherent textuality stands for the boundless and borderless capacity of creation and therefore satisfies the demands of the genre play.

Bibliography

Primary sources

Fitzgerald, F. Scott (1920). *This Side of Paradise*. New York: Scribner.
Fitzgerald, F. Scott (1925). *The Great Gatsby*. New York: Scribner's Sons.
Fitzgerald, F. Scott (1933). *Tender is the Night*. New York: Scribner.
Fitzgerald, Zelda (1932). *Save me the Waltz*. New York: Scribner.
Fowler, Therese Anne (2013). *Z: A Novel of Zelda Fitzgerald*. New York: Two Roads Group.
Gellhorn, Martha (1978). *Travels with Myself and Another*. London: Allen Lane,
Hemingway, Ernest (1926). *The Sun Also Rises*. New York: Scribner.
Hemingway, Ernest (1929). *Farwell to Arms* New York: Scribner.
Hemingway, Ernest (1952). *The Old Man and the Sea*. New York: Scribner.
Hemingway, Ernest. (1987). *The Complete Short Stories of Ernest Hemingway*. New York: Simon and Schuster, Inc.
Hemingway, Ernest (2010). *A Moveable Feast*. New York: Scribner.
McLain, Paula (2011). *The Paris Wife*. New York: Random House Publishing Group.
Robuck, Erika (2012). *Hemingway's Girl*. New York: Penguin Publishing Group.

Secondary sources

Abramson, J. (1996). Translation as Metaphor in Hildesheimer's Marbot Eine Biographie. *Paroles gelées, 14*(2). https://10.5070/PG7142003047. Retrieved from https://escholarship.org/uc/item/32687642.
Anderson, Benedict (1991). *Imagined Communities*. New York: Verso.
Azavedo, Carlos (1994). *Hemingway and Paris: The Cavalry of Woe*. Porto: Universidade do Porto. Faculdade de Letras.
Baker, Carlos (1968). *Ernest Hemingway: A Life Story*. New York: Charles Scribner's Sons.
Baker, Carlos (1972). *Ernest Hemingway: A Life Story*. New York: Penguin Books.
Baker, Carlos (2003). *Ernest Hemingway Selected Letters 1917–1961*. New York: Simon and Schuster.

Bakhtin, M.M. (1981). *The Dialogic Imagination: Four Essays*. Ed. Michael Holquist. Trans. Caryl Emerson and Michael Holquist. Austin and London: University of Texas Press.

Barry, Peter (2002). *Beginning Theory: An Introduction to Literary and Cultural Theory*. 2nd ed. Manchester: Manchester University Press.

Barth, John (1967). *The Literature of Exhaustion the Friday Book: Essays and Other Non-Fiction* (1984). London: The John Hopkins University Press. Retrieved from http://people.duke.edu/~dainotto/Texts/barth.pdf.

Barthes, Roland (1967). The Death of the Author. *Aspen No. 5–6*. Retrieved from http://www.ubu.com/aspen/aspen5and6/threeEssays.html.

Barthes, Roland (1975). S/Z. London: Cape.

Baudrillard, Jean (1988). *Selected Writings*. Ed. Mark Poster. Stanford, CA: Stanford University Press.

Benton, Michael (2009). *Literary Biography, an Introduction*. Chichester: Blackwell Publishing.

Benton, Michael (2015). *Towards a Poetics of Literary Biography*. London: Palgrave Macmillan.

Bertens, Willem Johannes, Bertens, Hans, & Fokkema, Douw (Eds.) (1997). *International Postmodernism: Theory and Literary Practice*. Utrecht: Utrecht University Press.

Beyer, E. London, & Liston, P. Daniel (1992). Discourse or Moral Action. A Critique of Postmodernism. *Educational Theory, 42*(4), 371–393. Retrieved from https://www.colorado.edu/education/sites/default/files/attached-files/Beyer_Liston_Discourse_or_Moral_Action.pdf.

Blanchot, Maurice (1999). *The Station Hill Blanchot Reader: Fiction and Literary Essays*. New York: Station Hill Press.

Boldrini, Lucia, & Novak, Julia (Ed.) (2017). *Experiments in Life-Writing*. London: Palgrave Macmillan.

Boldrini, Lucia (2012). Autobiographies of Others: Historical Subjects and Literary Fiction. Autobiographies of Others: Historical Subjects and Literary Fiction, 1–225. https://doi.org/10.4324/9780203112649.

Booth, Wayne C. (1961). *The Rhetoric of Fiction*. Chicago, IL: University of Chicago Press.

Brahm, G., & Driscoll, M. (1995). *Prosthetic Territories: Politics and Hypertechnologies*. Boulder, CO: Westview Press.

Bradford, R. (Ed.) (2018). *A Companion to Literary Biography*. Chichester: Wiley-Blackwell Publishing Ltd.

Bruccoli, J. Matthew (1994). *Fitzgerald and Hemingway: A Dangerous Friendship*. New York: Carroll & Graf.

Bruccoli, J. Matthew (2002). *Some Sort of Epic Grandeur*. Columbia: University of South Carolina Press.

Bruhn, J. Mark, & Donald, Wehrs R. (2014). *Cognition, Literature and History*. New York: Routledge.

Castellana, Riccardo (2015). Biofiction, Documnetality and the Internet. Metmorphoses of a Literary Genre. *The Mechanic Reader. Digital Methods for Literary Criticism LII (2015/2)*.

Cohn, D. (1990). Signposts of Fictionality: A Narratological Perspective. *Poetics Today*, *11*(4), 775–804. https://doi.org/10.2307/1773077.
Craig, Owens (1998). *The Allegorical Impulse – Toward a Theory of Postmodernism the Art of History: A Critical Anthology*. New York: Oxford University Press.
Culler, Jonathan (1997). *Literary Theory: A Very Short Introduction*. New York: Oxford University Press.
Currie, Mark (2013). *Metafiction*. New York: Rutledge.
Danova, Madeleine (2011). *The Jamesiad. Between Fact and Fiction: The Postmodern Lives of Henry James*. Sofia: Polis.
Davis, F. Tood (2006). *Postmodern (Midwestern) Morality: The Act of Affirming Humanity in a Screwed-Up World*. Albany: SUNY Press.
Dean, Ava (2017) *""To Be Novelized": An Investigation of Autofiction & How It Operates in Gwenaelle Aubry's No One"*. University Honors Theses. Paper 409.
Derrida, Jacques, & Ronell, Avita (1980). The Law of Genre. *Critical Inquiry*, *7*(1), 55–81.
Diliberto, Gioia (2011). *Paris without End: The True Story of Hemingway's First Wife*. New York: Harper Perennial.
Donaldson, Scott (1999). *Hemingway vs. Fitzgerald: The Rise and Fall of a Literary Friendship*. New York: Overlook Press.
Eagleton, Terry (1983). *Literary Theory: An Introduction*. Oxford: Blackwell Publishers.
Eakin, P.J. (1985). *Fictions in Autobiography: Studies in the Art of Self-Invention*. Princeton, NJ: Princeton University Press.
Eakin, P.J. (2008). *Living Autobiographically: How We Create Identity in Narrative*. Ithaca, NY: Cornell University Press.
Eco, U., & Eco, U. (1984). *Postscript to the Name of the Rose*. San Diego, CA: Harcourt Brace Jovanovich
Eco, U. (1983). *The Name of the Rose*. San Diego, CA: Harcourt Brace Jovanovich
Fitzgerald, F. Scott (2010). *F. Scott Fitzgerald: A Life in Letters: A New Collection Edited and Annotated by Matthew J. Bruccoli*. New York: Charles Scribner's Sons.
Foucault, Michael (1994). *The Archeology of Knowledge*. London and New York: Routledge.
Frye, Northrop (1957). *Anatomy of Criticism: Four Essays*. Princeton, NJ: Princeton University Press.
Frye, Northrop (1992). Henry James and the Comedy of the Occult. In Rutland Barry (Ed.), *Genre, Trope, Gender: Critical Essays by Northrop Frye, Linda Hutcheon and Shirley Newman* (pp. 5–33). Ottawa: Carleton University Press.
Genette, G. (1993). *Fiction & Diction*. Ithaca, NY: Cornell University Press.
Genette, Gérard (1992). *The Architext. An Introduction*. Berkley: California University Press.

George Moss, John Future (1987). *Indicative: Literary Theory and Canadian Literature.* Ottawa: University of Ottawa Press.

Goldschmidt, N. (2019). Afterlives of the Roman Poets. In P. Thonemann (Ed.), *Afterlives of the Roman Poets: Biofiction and the Reception of Latin Poetry* (Classics after Antiquity, p. I) (pp. 264–265). Cambridge: Cambridge University Press.

Grenz, Stanley J. (1996). *A Primer on Postmodernism.* Michigan: Eerdmans Publishing Co.

Griffin, M. Susan (1991). *The Historical Eye, The Texture of the Visual in Late James.* Boston, MA: Northeastern University Press.

Hawkins, A. Ruth (2012). *Unbelievable Happiness and Final Sorrow: The Hemingway-Pfeiffer Marriage.* Fayetteville: University of Arkansas Press.

Hawthorne, Nathaniel (1850). *The Scarlet Letter: A Romance.* Boston, MA: Ticknor and Fields.

Hemingway, Ernest (2003). *Selected Letters 1917–1961.* Ed. Carlos Baker. New York: Simon and Schuster.

Hemingway, Ernest 1899–1961 (1964). *A Moveable Feast.* New York: Charles Scribner's Sons.

Herman, David (2009). *Basic Elements of a Narrative.* Oxford: Blackwell Publishing.

Hotchner, A.E. (2015). *Hemingway in Love: His Own Story.* New York: St. Martin's Press.

Hutcheon, Linda (1985). A *Theory of Parody: The Teachings of Twentieth-Century Art Forms.* Urbana: University of Illinois Press.

Hutcheon, Linda (1989). *The Politics of Postmodernism.* London: Routledge.

Hutcheon, Linda (2003). *A Poetics of Postmodernism: History, Theory, Fiction.* New York and London: Routledge.

Kaplan, Cora (2007). *Victoriana: Histories, Fictions, Criticism.* New York: Columbia University Press.

Kress, Gunther (1988). *Communication and Culture: An Introduction.* Sydney: New South Wales University Press.

Kristeva, J. (1980). Word, Dialogue and Novel. In L.S. Roudiez (Ed.), *Desire in Language: A Semiotic Approach to Literature and Art* (pp. 64–91). New York: Colombia University Press.

Lackey, Michael (2021). *Biofiction. An Introduction.* New York: Routledge.

Lackey, Michael (2014). *Truthful Fictions. Conversations with American Biographical Novelists.* New York: Bloomsbury Academic.

Lackey, Michael (2016a). *The American Biographical Novel.* New York: Bloomsbury Academic.

Lackey, Michael (2016b). *Biographical Fiction. A Reader.* New York: Bloomsbury Academic.

Lackey, Michael. (2016c). Locating and Defining the Bio in Biofiction. *a/b: Auto/ Biography Studies, 31*(1), 3–10. https://doi.org/10.1080/08989575.2016.1095583.

Lackey, Michael (2021). *Biofiction: An Introduction.* New York: Taylor and Francis.
Layne, B. (Ed.) (2020). *Biofiction and Writers' Afterlives.* Newcastle: Cambridge Scholars.
Lejeune, P. (1989). *On Autobiography.* Ed. John Eakin Paul. Minneapolis: University of Minnesota Press.
Lejeune, Philippe (2009). *On Diary.* Eds. Jeremy D. Popkin and Julie Rak. Manoa: University of Hawaii Press.
Macey, David (2000). *The Penguin Dictionary of Critical Theory.* London: Penguin Books.
Makaryk, Rima Irene (1993). *Encyclopedia of Contemporary Literary Theory: Approaches, Scholars, Terms.* Toronto: University of Toronto Press.
Malpas, Simon (2005). *The Postmodern (The New Critical Idiom).* London: Routledge.
Marie-Luise Kohlke, & Gutleben, Christian (Eds.) (2020). *Neo-Victorian Biofiction. Reimagining Nineteenth-Century Historical Subjects* (p. 393). Leiden and Boston, MA: Brill Rodopi.
McAdams, Dan P., & McLean, Kate C. (4 June 2013). Narrative Identity. *Current Directions in Psychological Science, 22*(3), 233–238. https://doi.org/10.1177%2F0963721413475622.
McAdams, D.P. (2008). Personal Narratives and the Life Story. In Oliver P. John, Richard W. Robins, & Lawrence A. Pervin (Eds.), *Handbook of Personality: Theory and Research* (pp. 241–246). New York: Guildford Press.
McAdams, D.P., Josselson, R., & Lieblich, A. (Eds.) (2006). *Identity and Story: Creating Self in Narrative.* Washington, DC: American Psychological Association.
McFarland, Ron (2014). *Appropriating Hemingway. Using Him as a Fictional Character.* Jefferson, NC: McFarland & Company.
McHale, Brian (1988). Telling Postmodernist Stories. *Poetics Today, 9*(3), Aspects of Literary Theory, 545–557.
McHale, Brian (2003). *Postmodernist Fiction.* London: Methuen.
Middeke, Martin, & Huber, Werner (1999). *Biofictions: The Rewritings of Romantic Lives in Contemporary Fiction and Drama.* New York: Camden House.
Miller, Carolyn R. (1984). Genre as Social Action. *Quarterly Journal of Speech, 70*, 151–167; reprinted in Freedman & Medway (1994a, *op.cit.*), 23–42.
Miller, Carolyn R. (May 1984). Genre as Social Action. *Quarterly Journal of Speech, 70*, 151–167.
Mittel, Jason (2004). *Genre and Television (From Cop Shows to Cartoons in American Culture).* New York: Routledge.
Mizener, Arthur (1951). *The Far Side of Paradise: A Biography of F. Scott Fitzgerald.* Boston, MA: Houghton Mifflin.

Moses, Gabriel (1995). *The Nickel Was for the Movies: Film in the Novel from Pirandello to Puig.* Los Angeles: University of California Press.
Moulin, J. (2016). "Life Writing" n'est pas français: The Year in France. *Biography* 39(4), 606–614. doi:10.1353/bio.2016.0072.
Murphy, George (1989). *The Key West Reader, the Best of Key West Writers 1830–1990.* Key West, FL: Tortugas, Ltd.
Nancy, Milford (2013). *Zelda.* New York: Harper Perennial.
Natoli, Joseph, & Hutcheon, Linda (1993). *A Postmodern Reader.* New York: SUNY Press.
Novak, Julia Lajta (2011). *Biographical Fiction to Historiographic Metafiction: Rewriting Clara Schumann.* Brno Studies in English. Special Issue: Transgressive Auto/Biography, 37(2), 145–158.
Novak, Julia Lajta (2014). Nell Gwyn in Contemporary Romance Novels: Biography and the Dictates of 'Genre Literature'. *Contemporary Women's Writing,* 8(3), 373–390.
Nünning, Ansgar in Huber, Werner, Middeke, Martin, & Zapf, Hubert (2005). *Self-Reflexivity in Literature.* Wurtzburg: Königshausen & Neumann.
Onega, Susana, & Landa, Jose and Angel Garcia (2014). *Narratology: An Introduction.* New York: Routledge.
O'Sullivan, Tim, Hartley, John, Saunders, Danny, Montgomery, Martin, & Fiske, John (1994). *Key Concepts in Communication and Cultural Studies.* London: Routledge.
Prigozy, Ruth (2001). *The Cambridge Companion to F. Scott Fitzgerald.* Cambridge: Cambridge University Press.
Rademacher, Newhall Virginia (2022). *Derivative Lives: Biofiction, Uncertainty, and Speculative Risk in Contemporary Spanish Narrative.* London: Blumsbury Academic.
Ralph, Schneider, & Marcus, Hartner (2012). *Blending and the Study of the Narrative: Approaches and Applications.* Berlin and Boston, MA: Walter de Gruyter.
Renza, Louis A. (2005). Essay: *The Veto of the Imagination: A Theory of Autobiography.* UMI.
Reynolds, Stephen (1906). Autobiografiction. *Speaker,* 15(366), 28–30.
Reynolds, S. Michael (1989) *Hemingway: The Paris Years.* New York: W. W Norton and Company Ltd.
Sanderson, Rena, Spanier, Sandra and Trogdon, W. Robert e. (Eds.) (2015). *The Letters of Ernest Hemingway* (Vol. 3, 1926–1929). Cambridge: Cambridge University Press.
Sartre, Jean Paul (1948). *What Is Literature?* Paris: Gallimard.
Saunders, Max (2010). *Self-Impression: Life-Writing, Autobiografiction and the Forms of Modern Literature.* Oxford: Oxford University Press.
Schwob, Marcel (1924). *Imaginary Lives.* Trans. Lorimer Hammond. New York: Boni and Liveright.
Selden, Raman, & Widdowson, Peter (1993). *A Reader's Guide to Contemporary Literary Theory.* Lexington: The University Press of Kentucky.

Shelston, Alan (1977). *Biography*. London: Methuen.
Silbergleid, R. (2009). Making Things Present: Tim O'Brien's Autobiographical Metafiction. *Contemporary Literature, 50*, 129–155.
Skafidas, Michael (2019). Celebrating the Self, Remembering the Body: Desire, Identity, and the Confessional Narrative in Autofictional Verse. *ESC: English Studies in Canada, 45*, 85–113.
Slethaug, E. Gordon (1993). *The Play of the Double in Postmodern American Fiction*. Carbondale: Southern Illinois University Press.
Smith, Sidonie, & Watson, Julia (2010). *Reading Autobiography. A Guide for Interpreting Life Narratives*. Minneapolis: University of Minnesota Press.
Spanier, Sandra, Albert DeFazio III, J., & Robert Trogton, W. (Eds.) (2013). *The Letters of Ernest Hemingway Vol.2 1923–1925*. Cambridge: Cambridge University Press.
Stock, Noel (1970). *The Life of Ezra Pound*. San Francisco, CA: North Point Press.
Swales, J.M. (1990). *Genre Analysis: English in Academic and Research Settings*. Cambridge: Cambridge University Press.
Tate, Mary Jo (2007). *Critical Companion to F. Scott Fitzgerald: A Literary Reference to His Life and Work*. New York: InfoBase Publishing.
Todorov, Tsvetan (1975). *The Fantastic: A Structural Approach to a Literary Genre*. New York: Cornell University Press.
Todorov, Tsvetan (1976). The Origin of Genres. *New Literary History, 8*(1), 159–170.
Vermeulen, Timotheus, & van den Akker, Robin (2010). Notes on Metamodernism. *Journal of Aesthetics and Culture, 2*, pp. 1–14.
Vicars, James (2011). 'Storying' Lives: Biography as Story and the Ethical Imagining and 'Holding' of Lives. Ethical Imaginations: Writing Worlds Papers, the Refereed Proceedings of the 16th Annual Conference of the Australasian Association of Writing Programs, Australia.
Viljoen, Hein (Ed.) (2013). *Crossing Borders, Dissolving Boundaries*. Amsterdam: Rodopi Publishers.
Wagner-Egelhaaf, M. (2019). *Handbook of Autobiography/Autofiction*. Berlin and Boston, MA: De Gruyter. https://doi.org/10.1515/9783110279818.
Wales, Katie (1989). *A Dictionary of Stylistics*. London: Longman Publishers.
Waugh, Patricia (1984). *Metafiction (The Theory and Practice of Self-conscious Fiction)*. London and New York: Routledge.

Internet sources

Allen, M. (2017, April 07). Against 'Hybridity' in Genre Studies: Blending as an Alternative Approach to Generic Experimentation. *Trespassing Journal*, (2), Winter 2013. Retrieved from http://trespassingjournal.org/?page_id=488.
Baker, Allie (2010). *The Hemingway Project*. Retrieved from http://www.thehemingwayproject.com/happy-birthday-hadley/.

Beck, J. (2015, August 10). Life's Stories. How You Arrange the Plot Points of Your Life into a Narrative Can Shape Who You Are–And Is a Fundamental Part of Being Human. *The Atlantic*. Retrieved from http://www.theatlantic.com/health/archive/2015/08/life-stories-narrative-psychology-redemption-mental-health/400796/#article-comments.

Chandler, D. (1997). *An Introduction to Genre Theory*. Retrieved from http://www.aber.ac.uk/media/Documents/intgenre/chandler_genre_theory.pdf. Accessed May 22, 2018.

Daniel, Anne M. (2015, January 15). West of Hollywood: Stewart O'Nan on Fact, Fiction and F. Scott Fitzgerald. *The Huffington Post*. Retrieved from http://www.huffingtonpost.com/anne-margaret-daniel/west-of-hollywood-stewart_b_6471724.html.

Fischer, M. (2013, May 30). Saving Zelda. *The New Yorker*. Retrieved from http://www.newyorker.com/books/page-turner/saving-zelda.

Houston, Neal B. (1985). Hemingway: The Obsession with Henry James, 1924–1954. *Rocky Mountain Review of Language and Literature, 39*(1), 33–46. Retrieved from http://www.jstor.org/stable/1346761.

Internet Encyclopedia of Philosophy (2016). Retrieved from http://www.iep.utm.edu/lyotard/.

Jacobs, N. (1986). Michael Ondaatje and the New Fiction Biographies. *Studies in Canadian Literature / Études En Littérature Canadienne, 11*(1). Retrieved from https://journals.lib.unb.ca/index.php/SCL/article/view/8035/9092.

Josmall, Judy, & Reynolds, Michael. (2016). *Hemingway vs. Anderson: The Final Rounds*. Retrieved from http://mr2snob.tripod.com/sherwood_anderson/hemingway.htm.

Kakutani, M. (1999, November 30). With Hemingway as Friend, Who Needs Enemies? *New York Times*. Retrieved from http://www.nytimes.com/books/00/12/24/specials/fitzgerald-hemvs.html.

Kušnír, Jaroslav (2011). *Postmodernism in American and Australian Fiction*. Univerzitná knižnica Prešovskej Univerzity v Presov. Retrieved from http://www.pulib.sk/elpub2/FF/.

Lackey, M. (2016d, March 31). *The Uncanny Power and Artistry of Biofiction*. Bloomsbury Literary Studies. Retrieved from http://bloomsburyliterarystudies.typepad.com/continuum-literary-studie/2016/03/biofiction.html.

Lackey, Michael. *The Historical, Political and Literary Audacity of the Biographical Novel*. Writers and Artists. Retrieved from https://www.writersandartists.co.uk/writers/advice/665/a-writers-toolkit/style/.

Livescu, Simona (2003). From Plato to Derrida and Theories of Play, p. 7. *Comparative Literature and Culture, 5*(4). Retrieved from http://docs.lib.purdue.edu/clcweb/vol5/iss4/5.

Martin, E. (2011). Intertextuality: An Introduction. *The Comparatist, 35*, 148–151. University of North Carolina Press. Retrieved from https://muse.jhu.edu/issue/23460. Accessed June 29, 2018.

Nance, K. (2015, January 18). *Five Novels about Fitzgerald, Hemingway*. Retrieved from http://www.usatoday.com/search/Kevin%20Nance/.

Riesner, Ann-Marie, & Danneck, Martin (2015). Blending, Mixture, Hybridisation - Theoretical Approaches to Genre Blending. Conference Proceedings of: Poetik der Gattungsmischung / Poetics of Genre Blending. International Conference at Albert-Ludwigs-Universität Freiburg im Breisgau, in Cooperation with Ludwig-Maximilians-Universität Munich, March 27–29, 2014. Retrieved from http://www.jltonline.de/index.php/conferences/article/view/689/1587.

Saunders, M., 2019. Byatt, 'Fiction and Biofiction'. *International Journal for History, Culture and Modernity*, 6(1). Retrieved from http://doi.org/10.18352/hcm.543.

Schreibman, Susan, Siemens, Ray, & Unsworth, John (Eds.) (2004). *A Companion to Digital Humanities*. Oxford: Blackwell. Retrieved from http://www.digitalhumanities.org/companion/.

Schwalm, H. (2014) Autobiography. *The Living Handbook of Narratology*. Retrieved from https://www.lhn.uni-hamburg.de/node/129.html.

Sheppard, Robert. (1999). *The Necessity of Poetics*. Creative Writing Conference at Sheffield Hallam University. Retrieved from http://www.pores.bbk.ac.uk/1/Robert%20Sheppard, %20'The%20Necessity%20 of%20Poetics'.html.

Theriault, J. (2011, December 27). *Il Duce and Papa*. Retrieved from https://theamericanmag.com/il-duce-and-papa/.

Tranter, R. (2016, December 20). *Reading Biographical Fiction*. Interview with Michael Lackey. Retrieved from https://rhystranter.com/2016/12/20/michael-lackey-american-biographical-novel-interview/.

Trybulski, S. (2014, July 23). *The Hemingway Attack (Part IV). Something about Katy-Hemingway and John Dos Passos*. Retrieved from http://stantrybulski.com/2014/07/hemingway-attack-part-iv-something-katy-hemingway-john-dos-passo/.

Tuttleton, J. (1994, November). F. Scott Fitzgerald and the Magical Glory. *The New Criterion*. Retrieved from https://www.newcriterion.com/articles.cfm/F--Scott-Fitzgerald---the-magical-glory-5035.

Publications connected with this study

Krsteva, Marija, Donev, Dragan, & Kostova, Kristina (2019). Outline of Fictional Appropriations of F. Scott and Zelda Fitzgerald. Годишен зборник 2019- Филолошки факултет, Универзитет „Гоце Делчев" - Штип, 10 (14). ISSN 1857-7059.

Krsteva, Marija (2017). Fact vs. Fiction: The Doubling of the Biographical Self in Biofictions about F. Scott Fitzgerald and Ernest Hemingway. Conference Proceedings, Second International Scientific Conference "Filko" – Philology, Culture and Education. pp. 271–277. ISBN 978-608-244-469-7.

Krsteva, Marija (2016). Intertextual References to J. Conrad's Novella Heart of Darkness in F.F. Coppola's Film Apocalypse Now. Меѓународна научна конференција „Климентовото Дело". pp. 161–167. ISBN 978-608-244-404-8.
Krsteva, Marija (2016). Biographical Fictions about the Great American Authors F. Scott Fitzgerald and Ernest Hemingway. Conference Proceedings, First International Scientific Conference "Filko" – Philology, Culture and Education. pp. 439–448. ISSN 978-608-244-308-9. Conference "Filko" – Philology, Culture and Education. pp. 439–448. ISSN 978-608-244-308-9.
Krsteva, Marija (2015). Biofictions as Part of Contemporary Fiction. In: XII-а конференция на нехабилитираните преподаватели и докторанти от Факултета по класически и нови филологии, 15 May 2015, Sofia, Bulgaria. ISSN C633-2943. – Бр. 3.

MA and PhD dissertations

Buchberger, Michelle (2009). *Metafiction, Historiography and Mythopoeia in the Novels of John Fowles.* (doctoral dissertation). Brunel University School of Arts London, Great Bristian). Retrieved from https://bura.brunel.ac.uk/bitstream/2438/6558/1/FullTextThesis.pdf.
Forster, Iris (2011). *Postmodern Biofictions: Fictional Metabiographies by Antonia S. Byatt, Julian Barnes and Peter Ackroyd.* (MA thesis). University of Vienna, Vienna, Austria. Retrieved from https://core.ac.uk/download/pdf/11597333.pdf.
Hawkins, Christiane (2012). *Historical Metafiction and the Neo-Slave Narrative: Pastiche and Polyphony in Caryl Philips, Toni Morrison and Sherley Anne Williams.* (doctoral dissertation). Florida International University, Miami, Florida.
Kirchnopf, A. (2016). *Recent (Re)workings of (Post-) Victorian Fiction.* (doctoral dissertation). Eötvös Loránd University & Central European University, Budapest, Hungary. Retrieved from http://www.neovictorianstudies.com/past_issues/autumn2008/NVS%201-1%20A-Kirchknopf.pdf.
Krause, Jennifer A. (2009). *From Classical to Postmodern: Madness in Inter American Narrative.* (doctoral dissertation). Vanderbilt University, Nashville, Tennessee. Retrieved from https://etd.library.vanderbilt.edu/available/etd-07162009-155422/unrestricted/Dissertation.pdf.
Mandricardo, Alice (2010). *The End of History in English Historiographic Metafiction.* (doctoral dissertation). Scuola di dottorato in Lingue, Culture e Società. Venice, Italy. Retrieved from http://dspace.unive.it/handle/10579/1121.
Medzybrozsky, A. (2009). *Story and History: The Reconciliation of Realist and Postmodernist Approaches in Julian Barnes' Fiction.* (doctoral dissertation). Eötvös Lorand University. Budapest, Hungary. Retrieved

from http://www.julianbarnes.com/resources/archive/medzibrodszky.pdf.
Michler Bronwyn, Louise (2003). *Biographical Study of H. A. Junod: The Fictional Dimension*. (MA thesis). University of Pretoria, Pretoria, South Africa. Retrieved from https://repository.up.ac.za/bitstream/handle/2263/29174/00dissertation.pdf?sequence=1.
Szekely, Peter (2009). *The Academic Novel in the Age of Postmodernity: The Anglo-American Metafictional Academic Novel*. (doctoral dissertation). Budapest, Hungary. Retrieved from http://doktori.btk.elte.hu/lit/szekelypeter/thesis.pdf.
Von Dahlern, Nina Michaela (2012). *The Ethical Foundations of Postmodernity – Communicative Reality and Relative Individuals in Theory and North American Literature*. (doctoral dissertation). University of Hamburg, Hamburg, Germany. Retrieved from http://ediss.sub.uni-hamburg.de/volltexte/2012/5740/pdf/Dissertation.pdf.

Index

agency 40, 54, 55, 77, 82, 85, 96
allusion 25
A Moveable Feast 45, 82, 88–9, 92, 101, 104
Ann Fowler, Therese 4, 25, 46
architextuality 18
Aristotle 18
(auto)biofictional 3, 4, 6, 10, 12, 13, 19
autobiografiction 2, 18, 39, 106
autobiography 1, 2, 6, 13, 18, 37, 38–9, 49, 103, 105–6, 109
autofiction 2, 39, 103, 107
autotopography 2
autre-biography 2

Baker, Carlos 73, 84–5, 88–9, 101, 104, 107
Bakhtin, Mikhail 7, 16, 102
Barthes, Roland 9, 17, 102
bending 3, 90
bio 5, 31, 50, 55–6, 58, 90, 104, 106
biofiction 1, 2, 3, 4, 5, 6, 10–12, 14, 18, 19, 26, 28–31, 33–40, 42, 44, 49, 50, 61, 69, 71, 76, 78, 83, 90, 92, 96–8
biographee 2, 11, 36, 99
biographical fiction 1, 28, 30, 31–2, 36, 39, 43–4, 46, 47–9
biomythographies 3
biopreservation 4, 5, 6, 10, 11, 12, 13, 18, 35, 36, 37, 40, 41, 44–6, 49–55, 57–8, 61, 63–4, 67, 69, 72–82, 85–6, 89, 90, 93, 96, 98, 99, 103
biopreservational sequences 13, 35, 77

blending 3, 4, 5, 6, 12, 25, 28, 33–4, 36, 41, 76, 81, 99, 106–7, 109
boundaries 3, 37, 107
Bradford, Richard 32, 102

Castellana, Riccardo 26, 27, 102
Chandler, Daniel 7, 17, 108
coherent positive resolution 40, 58, 65, 75, 79, 81, 85, 96
collage 22, 23
communion 40, 59, 76, 81
contamination 40, 54, 55, 63, 75, 85

Danova, Madeleine 103
debunking 7
Derrida, Jacques 17, 103, 108
Diliberto, Gioia 71, 87, 103
Donaldson, Scott 53, 55, 57, 58, 103

Eakin 7, 40, 103, 105
element 10, 31, 34, 41, 50, 65, 58, 64, 76, 78, 83, 85, 89
exploratory narrative processing 40, 54, 64, 79, 87

factual metaautobiogrpahy 2
fake quotation 25
fictional biography 2, 31, 36, 37
Fitzgerald, F. Scott 4, 6, 7, 8, 9, 10, 11, 12, 13, 32, 36, 37, 42, 46, 48, 49, 50–2, 71, 79, 82–3, 85, 86, 92–3, 98, 99, 101, 102, 103, 105, 106, 107, 108, 109, 110
Fitzgerald, Zelda 13, 101

114 Index

frenemy 82
Frye, Northrop 7, 15, 16, 103

Gellhorn, Martha 4, 45, 88, 93, 94–6
Genette, Gérard 5, 6, 7, 17, 18, 22, 103
genre 3, 5, 14; *see also* genre play
genre play 3, 4, 5, 7, 8, 10, 11, 12, 14, 16, 18, 19, 22, 25, 31, 33, 50, 53, 69, 93, 97, 99; *see also* life-writing
Goldsmith, Nora 26
Greimas, A.-J. 9

Hartley, John 17
Hemingway, Ernest 4, 6, 8, 10, 42, 44, 45, 61, 66, 68, 73, 75, 77–9, 81–7, 98
Hemingway's Girl 4, 13, 45, 89, 96, 99
Herman, David 9, 10, 36, 40
heterobiography 2
historiographic metafiction 2, 3, 6, 8, 9, 24, 80–1
historiography 8, 31
Hodge, Robert 17
Hotchner, A.E. 44, 85–9, 91
Huber, Werner 26
Hutcheon, Linda 1, 4, 7–9, 21, 23–4
hybridization 3, 4, 5, 12

image-making 4, 11, 35
Interplay 2, 37, 49, 96–7
intertextual 3, 8, 11, 18, 40, 56, 58, 60, 62, 66, 71–2, 74, 77, 83, 85, 89, 91–3, 95, 99
intertextual parody 8, 60, 62, 66, 83
intertextual subtype 11, 40, 99
intertextuality 8, 9, 11, 22–3, 25, 54, 72–4, 76, 89, 97
irony 21, 23–5, 54, 56

jazz 47–8, 58

Kress, Gunther 17
Kristeva, Julia 18, 23
Kušnír, Jaroslav 9, 22–5

Lackey, Michael 28–33, 35
Layne, Bethany 26
life-writing 6, 7, 30, 32, 38–40, 96–7, 99; postmodern 3, 8, 11; genres 5;

genre-blending 12, 28 ; narratives 12; textuality 13, 97; genre play 1, 2, 3, 5, 13, 25, 27, 37, 97; investigation 36; illustration 37; intertextuality 97
literary biography 2–4, 7, 9, 12, 26–8, 34–6
literary modes 10, 22
literary symbolism 32
literary theory 1, 13, 14, 35
Lukacs, Georg 30

Mariella 89–93, 99
McAdams's, Dan. 9, 36
McFarland, Ron 42, 43, 44
McLain, Paula 4, 38, 41–2, 45, 70–9, 80–9, 90–1, 96, 98
McLean, Kate 9, 40
meaning-making 40
meta 4
metabiography 2, 36, 37, 39
metafiction 3, 8, 9, 22, 24–5, 33, 39–40, 80–1
metaxy 4
Middeke, Martin 26
Milford, Nancy 48
Miller, Carolyn 17
modernist 6, 7, 21–2
multi-genre 4

narrative identity 7, 9, 13, 18, 36–7, 39, 40–1, 50, 53–6, 64, 68–9, 70–1, 76, 78, 81–2, 93–4, 96–8
narrative 22, 29, 34, 35, 54; identity 18; techniques 19; genres 19; devices 24; modes 25; historical 27; biographical 28; form 30; elements 36, 40, 41; identity 36, 39, 40, 41, 50; autobiographical 40;
narrative sequences 1, 69, 78, 97
narratology 6, 9, 17
Nünning, Ansgar 7, 37–9

Onega et al. 9
O'Sullivan et al. 17

palimpsest 22, 51
paratextuality 18
parody 8, 23, 24, 25, 60, 62, 66, 78, 83
pastiche 8, 22–3, 25, 51, 62, 74, 92

Index 115

Pfeiffer, Pauline 32, 45, 64, 66, 73, 81, 85–91, 93–4, 99
Plato 4, 18–19
play *see* genre
postmodern parody *see* parody
postmodernism 4, 7–9, 14, 18, 20–4
post-postmodernim 7, 8
Pound, Esra 62, 64–5, 75, 79, 80, 82, 85
preservation *see* biopreservation
puppet master 33

quotation 8, 3, 25

redemption 40, 75
relativism 22, 24
rewriting 1, 5, 8, 22, 26, 39
Rhetoric 15, 16
Richardson, Hadley 6, 13, 32, 37, 39, 40–1, 45, 62–4, 66, 70–91, 93, 96, 98–9
Ricouer, Paul 9
Robuck, Erika 45–6, 89–93, 99

sacrifice 78–9
Saunders, Max 2, 7, 38–9
Save Me the Waltz 4, 13, 49–51, 56, 58, 59, 61, 67, 95, 98
Schwalm, Helga 7, 39

self-reflexive 1, 8, 9, 23
situatedness 83, 50–1, 53, 75
Stein, Gertrude 65, 75, 76, 79
Subverting 7, 8, 72
Swales, John 7, 16, 17

techniques *see* narrative; literary
textuality 1, 3, 4, 6, 9, 12, 13, 16–18, 35–7, 40, 45, 69, 97, 99
Todorov, Tsvetan 9, 15, 16
transtextuality 18
Travels with Myself and Another 4, 13, 94
triangle 63, 80, 85, 89–91
truth 11, 21–2, 29, 30, 32–5, 40, 46, 74–5, 92

UC 94–6
unit 10

Wales, Katie 17
Welsh, Mary 45, 94
White, Hayden 9
world making/world disrupting 52–3, 65, 67, 81, 85

Z: A Novel of Zelda Fitzgerald 4, 13, 37, 46, 49–79, 86, 98